WORLD'S YOUNGEST RELIGION

SIKHISM

Islamic Influence and Tibetan Connection

Mahinder N. Gulati
FIE, D.Phil.

ATLANTIC
PUBLISHERS & DISTRIBUTORS (P) LTD

Published by

ATLANTIC

PUBLISHERS & DISTRIBUTORS (P) LTD

B-2, Vishal Enclave, Opp. Rajouri Garden,
New Delhi-110027
Phones : 25413460, 25429987, 25466842

Sales Office
7/22, Ansari Road, Darya Ganj,
New Delhi-110002
Phones : 23273880, 23275880, 23280451
Fax : 91-11-23285873
web : www.atlanticbooks.com
e-mail : info@atlanticbooks.com

ISBN 81-269-0733-9

Printed in India
at Syndicate Binders, Noida

Preface

I feel great pleasure to place in the hands of readers the present booklet, which is no doubt small in size but large in substance. Before immigrating to the United States, I lived in Uttaranchal in the midst of the "land of gods", Deva Bhoomi, dotted with ashrams and numerous centres of worship, which ignited the philosophical spark in me to undertake this work.

The book is unique of its kind as it does not attempts to restate the usually known facts of Sikhism, rather it reveals those aspects with which the Sikh Sangat may not be generally familiar. Sikhism is the youngest of the world religions, dating back to 1469. It emerged as a reaction to the then particularistic tendencies of race, tribe, caste, etc. While Hinduism was at that time polytheistic, iconographic and ascetical, Islam was monotheistic, iconoclastic, socially motivated and practical. Sikhism sought to meet the contemporaneous challenges and motivate the people to target fresh goals of building a new society free from all evils of falsity about God, obscurantism and caste system. Such an ideology was initiated by Guru Nanak who held that God reveals and manifests himself through all in the universe, but no finite form can be worshipped as God, who is infinite. He propounded that all existence is controlled by one omnipotent, omnipresent and omniscient Lord called by different names–*Ishwar*, *Jehovah*, *Allah* and *Waheguru*. These are however known facts and almost all people of different religions have acquaintance with Guru Nanak and Sikhism as there is abundant literature available on Sikhism. The present book is distinct in the sense that it reveals and informs in depth of:

- Disposal of mortal remains of Guru Nanak, and its spiritual implications;
- Gurudwara "Pather Sahib" in the deep Himalayas in Leh-Ladakh;
- Concept of "Nanak Lama";
- Guru Nanak on a sort of Haj Pilgrimage to Mecca, Medina, Baghdad and other Muslim shrines.

Islamic influence on Sikhism particularly of the Sufi shade, and the profound veneration in which Guru Nanak is held by the Tibetans are indeed the *raison d'etre* for this book. I hope that the present book will be well-received by all readers as information provided here has been obtained from authentic sources and my extensive research in this direction.

I am thankful to Prof. K.R. Gupta, Chairman of Atlantic Publishers and Distributors (P) Ltd., New Delhi, for publishing this book in a record time.

3844 Woodside Terrace **Mahinder N. Gulati**
FREMONT CA 94539
USA

Acknowledgements

Although I follow Sikhism as a family-religion, I found myself lacking in doing full justice to this small book. Colonel Nirmal Singh, a close friend and an old colleague has rendered invaluable assistance in improving the manuscript for which I am profoundly grateful to him and his circle of Sikh friends.

Gurudwara "**Pather Sahib**" in the snowbound Himalayas is a landmark not only in the history of the Border Roads Organization of India but also throws new light on Guru Nanak's travels in that part of the world as well as his Tibetan connections. I am extremely grateful to Colonel S.S. Kahlon, Commander 16 Border Roads Task Force, for providing me the history of the events leading to the establishment of the Gurudwara and some beautiful picture to embellish this little book. Last, but not the least, I am grateful to Mrs. Vijay Suda for her painstaking proofreading and correcting the first draft.

Mahinder N. Gulati

Contents

Was Baba Nanak Cremated or Buried

1

Neither!

The story of Sikh Faith begins at Sultanpur where Baba Nanak received a vision to preach a way to enlightenment and God. Baba Nanak thereafter initiated a religious movement emphasizing what was common between Hinduism and Islam and preached the unity of the two faiths – a truly genuine secular movement to keep communal peace in the Indian sub-continent. Forcible conversions and killings of Hindus were a common occurrence. Guru Nanak preached Hindu-Muslim unity stressing that both belonged to the same land.

Guru Nanak's teaching about God is summed up in the Sikh 'Mūl Mantra', the creedal statement of Sikhism, which is equally applicable to Islam and Hinduism; hence the symbol '*Ek Onkar*' which stands for one primal reality:

> There is one God
> Eternal Truth is His name.
> Creator of all things and the all-pervading spirit
> Fearless and without hatred,
> Timeless and formless.
> Beyond birth and death,
> Self-enlightened.
> By the grace of the Guru he is known.

One of Guru Nanak's favorite metaphors which are common to Upaniṣads and Indian philosophical thought: he describes this world as an ocean, and liberation from it means to ferry the soul across to safety. The origin of this thought may lie in Buddhism. The omission of any reference to Christianity and Buddhism from Nanak's hymns is rather puzzling casting doubts if he went to Ceylon at all. From this sketchy evidence some researchers, particularly western, came to a hasty conclusion that Guru Nanak did not visit Ceylon, now Sri Lanka. However, historical evidence definitely leads us to the conclusion that Baba Nanak did visit Ceylon for which Rameshwaram was his base. In Sri Lanka Guru Nanak is remembered as *Sidh Nath* and *Ulag* Guru. And of course he certainly visited Tibet nearer home and Mecca-Medina-Baghdad across the proverbial 'seven seas'.

He went wandering about all over the countryside with the spirit of a seeker after Truth and Reality. His constant companions, Bhai Mardānā and Bhai Bālā, both Muslims, kept him company. They would go to a village only when they needed food. Legend has it that a rich banker, Rai Bhag invited Baba Nanak for a feast being given for the Brahmins. But the Baba refused to eat the food offered by Rai Bhag while at the same time he accepted food from a poor carpenter, Lalu. His explanation: The rich man's food was impure. He demonstrated the veracity of his statement by taking Rai Bhag's food in one hand and Lalu's in the other. As the Baba squeezed the food, drops of blood oozed out of Rai's food while milk poured out of Lalu's food. This incident was the basis of belief that Baba Nanak was endowed with magical or occult powers.

Unfortunately, Guru Nanak's attempts at uniting the two antagonistic communities proved a pipe dream, more so since the Sikhs were much closer to the Hindus. Nevertheless, Guru Nanak was revered both by Hindus and a large section of Muslim population of Punjab. He was a Saint for followers of both religions. When the Guru perceived in the manner of ancient Buddhist 'Rinpoché' (The 'Precious Ones') that the end was near, he himself appointed Bhai Lehna as his successor with title of Guru Angad. As Guru Nanak left for his heavenly abode, so great was the reverence for the Baba amongst his followers of all classes and creeds that a serious dispute ensued between the Hindus and Muslims. The Hindus wished to cremate the mortal remains of the Guru since he was born a Hindu, while the Muslims insisted on burial in the traditional Islamic manner for the simple reason that Guru Nanak preached from the Kora'n too, and had been a "*hāji*" in the sense that he had visited Mecca, Medina, Baghdad and many other pilgrimage centers sacred to the Muslims. Both parties were adamant. It is on record that while at Aden on his way to Mecca-Medina Guru Nanak was clothed in the dress of a *Hāji* going on a pilgrimage to Mecca. This just goes to prove that Baba Nanak was a Saint for all humanity rather than merely for the Hindus, later the followers of Sikh Faith.

Both Guru Nanak and Kabir thought on the same lines, so were their philosophies and teachings. To cap it all, there is almost complete similarity in the manner of their deaths and disposal of their mortal remains – Guru Nanak died on September 22, 1539, in the early hours of morning, an auspicious time of the day, amrit-vela, and the ambrosial hour. In the manner of spiritual masters of the Tibeto-Buddhism, the Guru knew that his time had come. The Muslim followers of the Guru wished to bury him while the Hindus wanted to cremate him since he was born a Hindu and died a Hindu. The Janamsakhis whose content is historical with a liberal doze of imagination are on record quoting the Guru telling the congregation: "You place flowers on either side, Hindus on my right and Muslims on my left. Those whose flowers remain fresh tomorrow will have their way." All those present were asked to pray after which the Guru pulled a sheet over him and went to eternal sleep. Next morning when the sheet was raised the congregation was totally flabbergasted; there was no sign of the Body! And the flowers of both communities were fresh as ever, which they reverently collected. No doubt, Guru Nanak was the Guru of the Hindus, Pir of the Musalmans and Lama for the Tibetans.

Baba Nanak was thus neither cremated nor buried. He was neither a Hindu, nor a Muslim saint in the Sufi tradition – this episode may sound like a mere myth, a tall-tale invented by the faithful to stress the religiosity or sanctity of Baba Nanak. But it might as well be an absolutely true statement of historical fact since similar instances have been recorded amongst the believers and advanced practitioners of Dzogchen, a system of mind-control and meditation that used to be prevalent in Tibetan Buddhism before the country was brutalized by Chinese communism.

When accomplished practitioners of Dzogchen perceived through their spiritual-clairvoyant powers that the end was near, they could bring their lives to an end at their will. They achieved this 'extraordinary and triumphant' end through deliberate will-power by letting their body to be reabsorbed back into its essential elements that created it. "Consequently, their material body dissolves into light and then disappears completely. This process is known as the 'Rainbow Body' or 'Body of Light' because the dissolution is often accompanied by spontaneous manifestation of light and rainbow." Sogyal Rinpoche, the renowned Tibetan spiritual teacher and author now settled in the West for over a quarter of a century, has cited a personally confirmed instance of this type of death, amongst others, that occurred in Eastern Tibet in 1952 when Sonam Namgyal, father of his Tutor, Jamyang Khyentse Chokhyi Lodro (1896-1959), attained this extraordinary dissolution of his mortal body. When he felt that his end was near, he requested to be left alone in a room, not to be disturbed at all, and his body not to be seen or touched in any way whatsoever for seven days. On the eighth day when members of the household entered the room there was no sign of the body except only his nails and hair. This famous instance of "Rainbow-Body" was witnessed by many other people too.

It will not be out of place to mention that the world renowned Sogyal Rinpoche runs numerous Rigpa Centers all over Americas, Europe, Africa and Asia to teach Tibetan spiritual techniques and has millions of followers and students – 'Rigpa' means "the Inner most nature of mind". His world famous voluminous Book, *The Tibetan Book of the Living and the Dying*, has sold millions of copies in nearly ten editions. Here it would be of interest to mention that in the Tibetan tradition, they do not celebrate birthdays of their exalted 'Masters'; instead they celebrate their death anniversaries, the moments of 'final illumination' of the Great Souls.

Founding of Sikh Faith

2

Guru Nanak Dev ji, Founder of the Faith, was born in a Hindu family on 15 April 1469 at village Talwandi Rai Bhoe, subsequently named Nankana Sahib, now in Pakistan, about sixty-five km north-west of Lahore. His father, Mehta Kalyan Das Bedi was a Patwari in that village, a sort of accountant in the revenue department of local administration. His mother's name was Mata Tripta. He had one elder sister, Bibi Nanki who, from Nanak's very childhood perceived in him the light of God. Indeed, Nanak was the embodiment of Divine Light but Bibi Nanki did not reveal the secret to any one.

The date of birth of Guru Nanak has been a subject of controversy, more so since even now his Birthday is officially celebrated on the full moon night of the month of November in accordance with Bālā *Janamsakhi*. Although most scholars do not agree with the *Janamsakhi*, official celebrations have continued to be held in November for the sake of tradition and continuity; however, there is no doubt that Baba Nanak was born on 15th April 1469, and this is a historical fact of which the Tibetans were aware of way back during the life times of the Guru; more about this later.

After Nanak received the Vision he went wandering about all over the countryside with the spirit of a seeker after Truth and Reality. His constant companions, Mardānā and Bālā kept him company. They would go to a village only when they needed food. Legend has it that that a rich banker, Rai Bhag invited Baba Nanak for a feast being given for the Brahmins. But the Baba refused to eat the food offered by Rai Bhag while at the same time accepting food from a poor carpenter Lalu: His explanation: The rich man's food was impure. He demonstrated the veracity of his statement by taking Rai Bhag's food in one hand and Lalu's in the other. As the Baba squeezed the food, drops of blood oozed out of Rai's food while milk poured out of Lalu's food. This incident gave rise to the belief that Baba Nanak was endowed with magical or occult powers.

Although Guru Nanak was the initiator of Sikh Faith, Sikhism as a religion took shape much later. Guru Nanak himself appointed Guru Angad as his successor. It was done during a congregation of Nanak's followers. The Great guru seated Bhai Lehna on his 'throne' and kept five paise and a coconut in front of him. Guru Nanak then bowed before Bhai Lehna and said to Bhai Buddha: "This is my successor, Guru Angad; put a tilak on his forehead in token of his appointment to the Guruship." Guru Nanak then informed the congregation that they should obey Guru Angad the same way as they did to him since "Guru Angad was in his own image".

> Guru Angad got the same tilak, the same umbrella over his head, and was seated on the same true throne as Guru Nanak. The seal of Guru Nanak's hand entered guru Angad's, and proclaimed his sovereignty.
>
> (Var I, pauri-45)

In other words, Bhai Lehna was just Bhai Lehna only, a mere human body; it was only after the ***JOT***, the Divine Light was installed in him by Nanak One that people bowed to him, as Guru Angad. Thus, Sikhs did not bow to the human body but to the JOT that was installed in that person. In turn, Guru Angad who left for his heavenly abode on March 29, 1552, installed Baba Amar Das in a repeat ceremony as the next Guru, with the remarks:

> Divine Light is the same
> Way and Mode are the same
> The Master has only changed the body.
>
> (Ramkali ki Var; Rai Balwand: p. 966)

In other words Guru Amar Das was treated as an avatar, an incarnation of Guru Angad. Once again, without saying so in so many words, the principle of Tibeto-Buddhist incarnation as applied to the line of Dalai Lamas is implied in the lineage of Sikh Gurus. Legend has it that when Nanak One left for his 'heavenly abode', no one found his body. Since Guru Nanak was not a mere human body; it was a JOT, a Divine Light, and his followers could not find his mortal remains as already narrated.

The influence of Tibeto-Buddhism on Sikhism is significant in another dimension. Sikh Gurus exercised supreme authority over religious, social and cultural affairs of the community. They were not dictatorial leaders of the Community; far from it. Nonetheless they were the highest spiritual authority till Guru Granth Sahib was accorded this highest honour. That precisely what was the practice in Buddhism, particularly the Vajrayana Buddhism that was prevalent in Tibet centuries before Sikhism appeared on the scene. Every Tibetan aspiring to study the scriptures had to have a 'Master', a Guru so to say, to guide the young student. Lord Buddha had said in one of the Tantras: "Of all the buddhas who have ever attained enlightenment, not a single one accomplished this without relying on a master, and of all the thousand buddhas that would appear in this aeon, none of them will attain enlightenment without relying on a master." It is a matter of conjecture whether the concept of a Sikh Guru as the supreme religious and spiritual authority originated with the Sikh Gurus themselves, or it was hang-over from centuries old tradition of Buddhism. In this connection it is of interest that Baba Nanak had visited what was then Tibet, and possibly North Sikkim too, then part of Tibet, where the practice of having a 'master' as spiritual teacher was obligatory.

In the later part of the fifteenth century Guru Nanak initiated a truly genuine secular movement to keep communal peace in the Indian subcontinent. However, the attempt at uniting the two antagonistic communities proved a pipe dream, more so since the Sikhs were much closer to the Hindus; in fact, they were the offshoot of Hindus. Nevertheless, the hymns of Adi Granth contain fair amount of knowledge of Islam and use the word 'Allah' numerous times. The *Kalima* too is mentioned. It is the affirmation:

"There is no God but God;
Muhammad is the messenger of God."[1]

In the same breath one may also mention one of Guru Nanak's favorite metaphors which are common to Upaniṣads and Indian

1. Adi Granth: 141.

philosophical thought: he describes this world as an ocean, and liberation from it means to ferry the soul across to safety. The origin of this thought and metaphor may lie in Buddhism. Kabir too was fond of this metaphor. Just as a fish does not feel it necessary to look for water, similarly a person who is one with God, immersed in God, does not feel it necessary to seek God since God is everywhere. One can catch echoes of Upaniṣads in Guru Nanak's hymns, couched in easy to follow popular local language.

The very first phrase of the Mūl Mantra is represented by the most significant words used in Sikh teachings: '*Ek Onkar*' – There is only ONE GOD. '*Ek Onkar*' stands for one primal reality. These are also the very first two words of Guru Granth Sahib, the most sacred Sikh scripture. While 'Ek' literally means ONE, Onkar is the equivalent of the Hindu 'OM' (AUM), the one syllable sound representing the holy Trinity of Brahma, Vishnu and Shiva – the God in His entirety. And what is OM: "That which the Vedas declare, that which all austerities utter, that in desire of which men become students, that word I tell you briefly is OM. That word is even Brahman, the Supreme."[2]

ੴ

In the same vein, Guru Nanak writes of Onkar:

The One Lord (Onkar) created Brahma,
The One Lord fashioned the human mind,

---

2. Kath Upaniṣad: 2-15.

From the One Lord came mountains and ages.
The One Lord created the Vedas.

(Adi Granth: 929)

Guru Nanak's teachings and precepts emphasize on Hindu-Muslim unity, equality of all human beings, crusade against Hindu caste-system and social evils, economic disparities amongst various sections of the people – all these together with the cruelties inflicted by the Muslim raiders/invaders, and a lot more, laid the foundations of what in due course developed into a powerful religious movement. Ultimately, it was the Tenth Nanak, Guru Gobind Singh who gave concrete shape to Sikhism as a distinct religious force whose primary objective was the protection of Hinduism against the atrocities and forced large scale conversions of the indigenous population to Islam, the religion of the invading hordes from the north-west.

Cultural Juxtaposition

3

In the Sikh view God is the Creator from whom all things and beings emanate. He is all-pervading. Most religions suggest that divinity exists deep within us, in our everyday experiences. That is immanence: God residing within us. This line of thinking is much too close to the Hindu belief, and far removed from the Islamic concept in which immanence of God in his creation, or the presence of God in man himself, is considered sacrilegious. On the other hand the concept that "God, the One, dwells within all, but is revealed only to him who receives his grace" which is almost identical to the Hindu view, would be acceptable to many followers of Sufism but certainly not to the Muslims at large. Here it should be remembered that Sikhs, Hindus, *et al.*, consider God as 'Sat', "Truth Eternal". He is the "Eternal Reality".[1] Nevertheless, God is without any attributes or qualities as such. How can the Creator be qualified? Since philosophically abstract concepts are beyond understanding by the masses at large, even Guru Nanak, like many other prophets, had to resort to attributing qualities to the Creator in order to give shape to abstract ideas. Be that as it may, Guru Nanak rejected the doctrine of '*avatar*' as propounded by Lord Krishna in the Gita, although Krishna qualified his 'avatarhood' as quite sophisticated with the words –

> Though unborn, the Imperishable Self,
> And also the Lord of all beings brooding over nature,
> Which is Mine own,
> Yet I am born through My own Power.

(Bhagavad Gītā: IV-6)

---

1. Adi Granth: 931.

Hence the Guru's Mūl Mantra:

> Timeless and formless
> Beyond birth and death.

The partition of India in 1947 followed by massive unprecedented transmigration of populations on a scale hitherto unheard of in the annals of civilization, once again brought forth the fundamental cultural unity of Hindus and Sikhs[2]. Of course Sikhs were not classified as Hindus; they are not Hindus, and Hindus are not Sikhs either. It is the same cultural springboard, similarities in doctrines and dogmas – these are the points at issue. Furthermore, there is a subtle difference between the Sikh-Hindu concept of avatar and the Buddhist doctrine of Incarnation, or Tibeto-Buddhist Doctrine of Reincarnation, birth and rebirth. After all, the Sikhs too believe in rebirth and Karma as do the Hindus. To deny the doctrine of Karma would indeed be hypocrisy on the part of Sikhs, Hindus and the allied sects.

Death and funeral ceremonies among the Sikhs and Hindus are almost identical. Cremation is the rule. The doctrine of rebirth or incarnation does not in any way preclude cremation of the mortal remains. On the other hand, Muslim's belief in the bodily resurrection made burial obligatory; cremation was out of the question. Guru Nanak's views on this controversial question are couched in diplomatic language and are recorded in the Adi Granth, 466:

> The clay of a Muslim's grave falls into a potter's clod. From it vessels are fashioned and bricks made. It cries out as it is burnt. The poor clay burns and weeps and the fiery ash continually falls from it. Nanak says: God the Creator who made the world, alone knows whether it is better to cremate or to bury.

It really does not matter whether one believes in cremation or burial; it is more important to be true to one's religion and beliefs. And who is a true Muslim? In the eyes of Guru Nanak a true Muslim is he who sees truth in the religion of others. Conceit in one's religion does not make one a truly religious person. Since

2. Sikhs constitute approximately 2% of Indian population with maximum concentration of about 60% of them in Punjab State.

resurrection is the primary rationale behind burial as the accepted way of disposing off the mortal remains of a Muslim, it stands to reason that life would once again return to the buried body. In other words a sort of rebirth would take place, albeit as a replica of the dead person, usually fully grown up. If this hypothesis is conceded, acceptance of rebirth, and consequentially incarnation in one form or another, appear to be universally accepted doctrine, in implied sense if not directly. It will thus be seen that Islam was portrayed by Guru Nanak as a path by which Truth could be reached. Guru Nanak accepted the religious language of Hinduism and Islam when it suited him, but the Truth that he expressed was always his own:

> Baba Allah is inscrutable. He is boundless. His abode is holy and so are His names. He is the true sustainer. His will surpasses comprehension. It cannot be adequately described. Not even a hundred poets coming together could describe the smallest part of it. All hear and talk about Him, none fully appreciates His worth.
>
> (Adi Granth: 141)

Islamic theology has been explained by Guru Nanak in his hymns compiled in the Adi Granth. The vocabulary may be different, but teachings of the Mūl Mantra are not lost sight of: the two appear to be almost identical, showing thereby how close to Islam were Guru Nanak's thoughts:

> Allah is ineffable; He is inscrutable; He is the all-powerful Creator, the Merciful. The whole world is transitory and the Merciful alone is permanent. Only He is eternal, for he is not subject to any destiny. The earth and the heavens shall perish; only he, the only One, remains for ever.
>
> (Adi Granth: 64)

In a major departure from Hinduism, Guru Nanak introduced the concept of "*grhastha* sannyasin" as a significant social reform. All four stages of life as laid down in Hindu *Sastra* were merged into one. And he did so by personal example as well as precept. One did not have to give up the world and family life to seek '*Moksha*' in the jungles, or go to mountain tops to do '*Tapasya*' to seek God; this could, and should, be achieved by living full life performing one's social and religious duties. Concurrently, Guru Nanak abolished all caste distinctions which were a bane of Hindu society, particularly the scourge of untouchability. Every one was a servant of God. Guru Nanak thereby reinterpreted Hinduism in terms of a single unified society in which every person was equal as he was in the eyes of God. It could therefore be safely concluded that Guru Nanak pre-empted, anticipated by 2-3 centuries the social reforms later brought forth by Arya Samaj. His social reformist campaign was indirectly aimed at putting a stop to conversion of Hindus to Islam. This was also an attempt to bring the two major communities, Hindus and Muslims, to come closer and live together. "There is no Hindu and no Musalman"; the one God transcends both and can be reached through either path, both leading to the same destination. By this the gurus did not mean to denounce either religion as false, or any other religion for that matter. However, the cultural aspects of Hinduism were either rejected or dismissed with the result that Sikhism landed itself in the same boat as Buddhism or Christianity in as much as it had practically no cultural moorings of its own.

Ethical monotheism is the basis of working relationship with other religions. Incidentally, the present differences between Sikhs and Muslims stem more from socio-political grounds and the tragic events of 1947 rather than on theological considerations.

No set of religious traditions and dogmas can be valid for all times to come. Change is the essence of life, even though the fundamentals may remain unchanged. A certain degree of reinterpretation may be necessary, but once again the fundamentals remain constant. Of late, the Sikh youth had considerable exposure to western culture. Now they find it difficult to identify themselves with rustic Punjab and its rather crude rural cultural environment. So where to go?

> There is no other place to go except God; He is but one.
>
> (Adi Granth: 60)

The true Hindu or Muslim is one who transcends the faith. It is not that Guru Nanak was attempting to produce some sort of mutually acceptable theological synthesis; far from it. As far as he was concerned, he may have regarded both Hinduism and Islam as false. If that was so, then Sikhism too was false and unnecessary.

However, Guru Nanak was a practical man. He felt the need for men to congregate together and collectively strive for spiritual development and sustenance. Thus, all that he was trying to create was a certain harmonious social lifestyle under which the two communities could reconcile to each other to live in peace. Guru Nanak believed in "social religion" and an individual soul, and also in a mystical heavenly *sangat*. Unfortunately, the Guru's criticisms of *Brahmanical* Hinduism went against the vested interests of the high caste Hindus who regarded '*varnashramadharma*' as sacred. They were not prepared to accept equality with the lower caste Hindus, let alone with the Muslims whom in any case they considered as impure. In the same vein Guru Nanak condemned the ritual aspect of religion when he says:

> A man washes his clothes and his body and thinks that automatically he has become pure, ignorant of the filth attaching to his inner self he rubs and cleans himself externally, without realizing that our outer senses may deceive us; our memory may be an illusion.
>
> All means of knowledge exist only as dependent on self-experience and since such experience is its own proof there is no necessity for proving the existence of self. In any case it cannot be proved because it is the basis of all proof. The self is self-established and is different from all else, physical and mental. It is undifferentiated consciousness. It remains unaffected even after the person dies and the body is reduced to ashes and the mind perishes.

"The Self (*Ātman*) is existence, knowledge and bliss." The Ātman is universal and infinite. There is no absolute existence; it is all relative in nature. Guru Nanak always stressed cleansing of the inner self; he preached simple living and high thinking. Guru Nanak's basic lesson in social religion:

> There is no Hindu and there is no Musalman.
> He who deems that both the ways lead to the one Lord,
> Shall be emancipated.

(Adi Granth: 142, 223)

> From the one Lord all are born. The routes are two, but know that their master is one. Under the Guru's instruction,

> recognize his order. Says Nanak, I praise the one Lord who is contained in all shapes, colors and beings.

This was the essence of Guru's attitude to religions of the day. He argued that since God is One – God is not only One but 'One without a second one' – of necessity therefore paths laid down by Hinduism, Islam and various other religions must all converge at the same goal, the One God. 'His monotheism verges on monism, and sometimes little space appears to be left for human free will.' Guru Nanak firmly believed that Man is only a part of the Cosmos; it is the unity of God that is supreme. The trouble with such religious thoughts that pushed the individual to duality rather than unity was a threat to social harmony. Freedom from fear of dragons and demons, the 'supernatural' magical cults, superstition, and all such evil thoughts were serious obstacles towards achieving the goal of oneness with God. In this respect Guru Nanak's philosophy was simple and straight-forward. Neither a new theological vocabulary was invented by Guru Nanak, nor any doctrinal innovations introduced by him. Simple living, high thinking: that was Guru Nanak personified; for him, liberation depended on an inner experience of God.

Guru Nanak's attitude to religion in his youth is illustrated by some anecdotes:

> Mardānā was a '*mirasi*' by caste, a street-singer, a low caste 'shudra'. His original name was Dana. He was a constant companion of Guru Nanak. In order to improve their social status the mirasi caste had converted to Islam. Guru Nanak invited Mardānā to be his companion and to set his hymns to music. Mardānā declined: How could a 'shudra' be a friend of a 'Kshatriya'?
>
> "We are both human beings. God created us equal." Mardānā was thus persuaded to join Guru Nanak.

In another instance the Guru's party came across a group of ascetics in the forest. Nanak asked their leader, Santrain, why they wore no clothes. Santrain informed the Guru that they were seekers after 'nirvana' and had therefore renounced everything including clothes. They had no possessions, and no home or hearth. When questioned about the source of food, Santrain replied that they ate whatever they received in charity. Nanak then offered money which his father had given him for trading. Santrain declined. Nanak then went away, bought some food, but even that was refused by Santrain. When his companions questioned him why he had refused the food, he informed them that Nanak was God himself – in other words, an avatar or incarnation of God Himself; it was not in the fitness of things that God Himself should serve the yogis. In fact the God had come to see how the yogis were faring.

> This brings us to another concept of Sikhism – that of fellowship coupled with consolidation, permanence and distinctiveness. A Sikh could not be a purely private person.

However, it is a different matter altogether that the Partition of India in 1947 almost undid all their efforts to avoid extinction by the Moghuls and to maintain their separate identity, and instead put the Sikhs on track for re-absorption in Hinduism. But subsequent political developments re-established the distinct identity and status of the Sikhs; however, this aspect is beyond the scope of this work.

Mysticism

4

Guru Nanak was a mystic.

In the distant past, mysticism as a spiritual concept was prevalent primarily amongst the eastern intellectuals and philosophers. It was sort of *infra dig* in the West. However, with the spread of religious thought in a refined form, it is no longer considered an esoteric system. On the contrary, mysticism has gained a respectable position as one of the highest expressions of religious thought. In fact practically all religious movements have taken shape out of mysticism of one sort or the other. Not only that, practically all world religions trace their origins to the mystic experience of their prophets. However, the validity of mystic experience has to be made sure before we accept the same at its face value, while at the same time true mystics must not be dubbed as heretics. The latter possibility cannot be ruled out since personal and direct experience of Reality is the very basis of mystic's pronouncements. Despite worldwide acceptance of the concept, it is difficult to arrive at an all-round acceptable definition of mysticism, more so since "we fail to distinguish the simple facts of religion from the accounts which reach us through the depths of theological preconceptions. Experiences of St. Theresa about the Trinity or of St. Paul hearing the voice of Jesus while walking the Damascus road, and numerous others from practically every region or religion of the world may be cited as examples. Thus there may be as many varieties of mysticism as there are religions and sects. However, there is general agreement on principal varieties of mysticism; these are:

- **Nature Mysticism** is the elementary stage of mysticism in which a person feels identity with objects of Nature as opposed to the Supreme Creator, or God. He feels one with nature and its objects. However, the mystique does not deny existence or supremacy of God but considers Him as higher and above Nature, an altogether different superior entity. Nature Mysticism is neither a higher consciousness, nor a higher or monastic mysticism. It has nothing to do with morality, or moral aspect of one's actions. It is this characteristic that distinguishes Nature Mysticism from Theistic Mysticism, the starting point for Divine Mysticism. While Nature Mysticism seeks to form oneness with Nature, Sikh Mysticism aspires in the opposite direction "to control and eliminate the raw and disharmonious functioning of the natural consciousness or the egoistic aspect of the psyche".

- **Isolationist Mysticism** is essentially dualistic in nature comprising of spiritual and material elements. It is completely divorced from Nature Mysticism which may be interpreted as the illusory Māyā. Buddhism, Jainism, *Sankhya* or Yoga, do not believe in God as envisaged in Theism. It, therefore, stands to reason that 'isolation mysticism' is almost identical with Monistic Mysticism, "as distinct from Pluralism or Dualism." After the soul is withdrawn from the temporal world, it hardly matters whether "the soul lies isolated in its own essence, or is a part of the Non-functioning Quality-less Brahman, Void or *Shunyata*". Some worship avatars, perform rites and do pilgrimage to seek deliverance, while others seek God through Bhakti – devotion to God as well as to Guru, the Teacher. The very name 'Sikh' is derived from the word '*Sisya*', a disciple. The Bhakti, loving devotion for God and Guru is the very basis and root of Sikh religion. Historian and scholars are, therefore, led to the conclusion that Sikhism is a syncretistic religion, a reconciliation of diverse opposing religious views – a synthesis of Bhakti movement within Hinduism and Sufi philosophy of Islam. Nevertheless, Sikhism is neither Hinduism nor Sufism, having unique postulates that are quite different from both.
- **Monistic Mysticism**: Once again, there is no idea of God in Monistic Mysticism, nor is there any scope for love

and devotion as it is in 'Theistic Mysticism'. However, asceticism is a common undercurrent since the goal is the same – complete isolation from the temporal world so as to be free from the worldly affairs, and achieve eternal bliss, tranquility beyond and above good and evil – *Nirvana* in other words as opposed to *Samsara*. That is why withdrawal from the worldly pleasures (and pain) is *sine qua non* for reaching Monistic Mysticism, and to that extent, it is identical with asceticism. It is noteworthy that Sikhs and their founder Guru Nanak hold that beings are caught in the whirling wheel of samsara – of involuntary births and deaths – because of self-identification with the body and its environment.

- **Theistic Mysticism** accepts a beneficent God. Worship of a deity, love and devotion are its intrinsic elements. The mystic considers life as an unnecessary involvement and a burden. His final goal is merger in God which he aspires to achieve through ascetic or ritualistic practices and meditation. A variation of this is the 'Theistic Mysticism of Union' in which the mystics accept the distinction between God and soul of the subject. They follow the path of withdrawal so as to achieve union, and not mere merger, with Universal Soul. Christian mystics, Sufis and some *Saivites* follow this line of thinking. However, semi-active Theistic Mystics belong to the class of mystics who are not so other-worldly.
- **Prophetic or Activity Mysticism**: For the followers of this line of mysticism, God is the Creator of this world, but He is distinctly different from His Creation, nor is He the material cause of this world. The crux of mysticism is: "God is love, and the object of love." An 'ordinary mystic' and the 'prophetic mystic' have distinctly different perceptions of their mystic experiences and consciousness. The latter has a "functional union' with God since he has a specific message to deliver, besides developing a higher spiritual consciousness, more so since "Mysticism by its very definition and nature is a direct personal and extra-sensory experience of Reality".

The Christian-Protestant Mysticism believes that Divine Life and Light are within man himself. "The Kingdom of God is within you and he who searches for it outside of himself will never find it.... God is within us and is waiting for us to return to Him."

***Samkhya* Mysticism** follows more or less the above precepts of Jainism, which we need not elaborate any further. Similarly, **Yoga** is not a new metaphysical system either; it is only a different means to the same end – peace of mind to gain power to rid the human body-soul of bondage and suffering; total freedom from the bondage of life-cycles and the sufferings it involves. The next phase after preparing the body for rigors of asceticism is the control of the **Mind** through concentration on a single point or object, whatever that may be. It is meditative phase at its best, eliminating the duality that existed between the mind and the object or point of concentration.

Vedic Mysticism: The Vedic religion was essentially a ritualistic sacrificial type, and to that extent it does not fall in the category of mysticism. However, since Vedic knowledge is non-sensory and non-rational, the system has been called 'mysticism'. The Rig Veda is the fundamental Veda comprised of about 1028 hymns, all in praise of elements of Nature like fire, rain, sun, wind, etc. Most of these hymns are in the nature of worship of the deities of Nature for material benefit of the community at large, seeking prosperity, health and long life for the people and cattle. In this respect these are fundamentally on the same lines as the hymns of Guru Granth Sahib. Since the chief Vedic God was Indra, a major portion of the hymns are addressed to god Indra. A significant characteristic of the Vedic system has been that it absorbed and expanded with new amalgamation of fresh ideas, rituals and religious concepts, while at the same time its inability to discard old tenets proved its strength and durability. One might as well go a step further to say that Hindu religion and culture absorbed the impact of fresh assaults and embraced them as if they belonged to the indigenous soil. In the process, Hinduism was no longer a religion as such, but more of a way of life taking in its fold all that came its way so long as the incoming hordes were willing to do so. In short, Vedic religion was clearly polytheistic for the simple reason that its gods were merely personification of forces of nature – obviously, a hangover from primitive days when what could not be comprehended was thrown into the well of divinity. However, "in Sikhism the doctrine of incarnation (Avatar), or God taking the human form, is strictly denied and is considered heretical...." But that cannot be taken as the last word on incarnation or reincarnation since Avatar is not necessarily limited to the interpretation taken herein. Incarnation need not necessarily be restricted to God taking the form of Man; it could be incarnation of one man unto another. It is in this Tibeto-Buddhist context that the doctrine of incarnation may be considered applicable in Sikhism; and hence Nanak I to Nanak X. All the same, Sikhism is a strictly monotheistic system. The same holds good in case of Christianity too.

In all fairness it must be explicitly stated that the Gurus strongly repudiated the theory of incarnation. Sikhism does not accept that man merges in God. To say that man merges in God and god takes the human form tantamount to one and the same thing. Once again it needs to be noted that the Gurus repudiated the theory of Avatarhood; incarnation is certainly not restricted to God taking the human form. The concept and practice of Incarnation or Reincarnation as espoused in Tibeto-Buddhism is far wider in its scope and application. In the same vein it might as well be clarified that Guru Nanak did not have a living Guru. When he uses the word 'Guru' in his hymns, he means God, and not another human being as his Guru. "Listen, the Eternal God Lord is my Guru.... I salute the Primeval Lord, the Guru, who was in the beginning and before the ages began.... My *Sat Guru* is eternal; he is neither born nor dies."

Islamic Mysticism: "Allah is One, all things depend upon Him; He begetteth not, and He is not begotten; and there is none like unto Him." While stressing the duality, the Kôra'n makes a clear cut distinction between man and God who is Transcendent, notwithstanding His immanent aspect. This latter attribute became the bone of contention and led to persecution of the Sufis by the Orthodox Muslim Church so much so that, in some cases, the latter refused to even recognize the Sufis as Muslims. This just shows how emphatically theistic Islam is, perhaps the first world religion to do so, the credit for which goes to Prophet Mohammad. The salient features expressed in the Kôra'n are 'unity of human origin and brotherhood of man', particularly so in the human and moral fields. The early leaders of Islam like Prophets Umar Ali, Usman and Abu Bakar set the highest standards of human conduct. Thus primacy of moral life in society was considered as the keystone towards progress of human race. Equality, solidarity and freedom are considered the foundations of all moral life. Islam, like Sikhism makes no distinctions between secular life and religious life. The empirical and the spiritual carry the same connotation with the result that there is no bifurcation between the Church and the State. The Kôra'n unites religion and the state, ethics and politics. Theoretically speaking, a person is loyal to God, and not to a King or the State. In this respect there is a fundamental difference between classical Islam and Sufism – worldliness of the former and other-worldliness of the latter are obviously at divergent ends. That in itself is the source of sectarian conflict between the two schools of thought. Nonetheless, Christianity continued to maintain the division between the secular and spiritual segments of life and administration. On the other hand, compositions by Sri Chaitanya, Tulsidas or Mirabai are absent from the compilation of Guru Granth Sahib so that Sikhism and Sikh society steers clear of esotericism and mysticism of austerities and self mortification and the general negativism of such cults and sects. Guru Nanak succeeded in his mission because he had a clear vision of his social purpose. He wanted his Faith to continue and develop further. That is why he appointed his spiritual successor, another Guru, but not his son, to take his place after his death. Continuity of social and religious reformist movement was his primary concern, and not to create a family legacy. This also set in place a system whereby the institutional framework was strengthened for future development. Authentication of the scriptures by Guru Arjun and finally the creation of the *Khalsa* by Nanak X was the culmination of Guru Nanak's forethought. The history of the *Khalsa* may therefore be broken down into the following six phases:

1. **Phase 1**: The period prior to the emergence of the Khalsa; begins with the death of the Fifth Guru in 1606.
2. **Phase 2**: Period of Guru Gobind Singh 1675-1708; 1699 was the critical year when the Khalsa was actually founded.

3. **Phase 3**: Period following the death of Guru Gobind Singh.
4. **Phase 4**: Period of great suffering and persecution inflicted by the declining Mughal power; execution in 1716 of Banda, the military successor to Guru Gobind Singh.
5. **Phase 5**: Period of triumph; formation of eleven large misls. Ranjit Singh got control of Lahore in 1799 and was formally invested with the title of Maharaja in 1801.
6. **Phase 6**: The climax; period of unification of the Sikh State.

Banda Bahadur

5

Banda was born of Rajput parents in 1670 at Rajouri (Poonch) with the name of Lachman Das. He joined an order of mendicants (*bairagis* in Punjabi) at an early age and was given the name of Madho Das. He took to asceticism and set himself up in a hermitage on the bank of river Godavari in South India and lived at Nanded for more than 15 years before he met Guru Gobind Singh who charged him with the sacred task of punishing those who had persecuted the Sikhs and murdered his sons. Lachman Das described his relationship with the Guru as that of *banda*, a slave, and that is the name the Guru gave to Lachman Das: Banda to be later known as Banda Bahadur, the military Hero. Guru Gobind Singh honored Banda with five arrows from his quiver, gave him his own standard and battle drum, thereby virtually declaring Banda as commander of all Sikh forces which position Banda assumed for himself in course of time by virtue of his military successes. The Guru also issued a *hukamnama* (official orders) for all Sikhs urging them to volunteer for military service.

Banda proceeded towards north with a small band of followers. While in the vicinity of Delhi Banda learnt that Mughal Emperor Bahadur Shah was still in the Deccan involved in fratricidal war with his own brother over succession to the throne of Delhi. Finding this just the right opportunity, Banda planted the Guru's standard in a village about 60 km from Delhi and exhorted all Sikhs to join his force in compliance with the Guru's *hukamnama*.

Asceticism and denial of self was in Banda's blood. Whatever his forces plundered he gave away to the poor and needy. People flocked to his congregations with offerings of goods and money which again Banda gave away to the people at large. His reputation spread, and with that more and more money, goods and volunteers came to his camp. Banda now issued a proclamation offering protection to any one who was persecuted on religious grounds, or otherwise threatened by Muslim bigots, or any one else for that matter. This is what the peasants of Punjab were looking forward to. They rose in revolt against injustices inflicted on them by *zamindars* and local officials, Muslims or Hindus alike. And Sirhind was of special significance not only to Banda alone but also to the entire Sikh community, besides of course to the Guru himself.

It may be recalled that Guru Gobind Singh had three wives: Bībī Gīto, Bībī Sundri and Bībī Sahib Kaur who gave him four sons – Ajit Singh, Jujhar Singh, Zorawar Singh and Fateh Singh. The elder two, Ajit Singh and Jujhar Singh attained martyrdom in 1704 at Chamkaur Sahib (Battle of Chamkaur) in district Ropar (Punjab) while the younger two were bricked alive at Sirhind the same year under orders of Wazir Khan, the Mughal Governor of Sirhind. The Guru faced the personal tragedy bravely, and wrote:

> Chār moye to kya hua, Jeewat keyi hazār.
>
> "So what if four have died; thousands are still alive."

Banda grabbed his moment of fate and ordered his peasant army to march towards Sirhind. A number of towns were laid waste en route. The captured booty from the government treasuries and wealthy landlords was distributed amongst the Sikh soldiers and public at large. The Mughal Subedar Wazir Khan decided to take a stand about ten miles outside Sirhind where the two unequal armies faced each other on May 14, 1710. The Mughal force was equipped with a number of cannons who opened up on the peasants. Banda and his brave men were imbued with a spirit of revenge. They charged the firing-cannons fearlessly. A hand to hand fighting ensued. Banda had the advantage of preponderance of numbers. Wazir Khan was killed in action and his army of horsemen and footmen retreated towards Sirhind, chased by the peasant army, wielding their swords ruthlessly and liberally, which was their principal armament. Hardly any soldier of Islam escaped alive. Dewan Sucha Nand who was instrumental in execution of Guru's two sons was captured alive.

Banda stormed the town of Sirhind which he entered on May 24, 1710. Almost nothing was left standing in this small but notorious town. All were laid waste. The palace of the Subedar and treasury of the Dewan yielded rich booty which was liberally distributed amongst the victorious peasants. In the process Banda the *bairagi* became Banda Bahadur, master of all the territories between the Yamuna and Sutlej rivers. A number of Muslims and Hindus voluntarily embraced the Sikh Faith. Soon the tract between Sutlej and Ravi rivers was over run by Banda's armies. With Amritsar as the base, they captured Batala and Pathankot looting and plundering all townships en route. It is noteworthy that Amritsar was the chief trading center of Northern India where caravans laden with precious and attractive goods from Central Asia exchanged them for the product of India. It was indeed a city of wealth and splendor. However, it was not one city; its different parts were owned by wealthy families who had built fortresses in which they maintained mafia-type gangs who acted like tax collectors. They harassed the business community and demanded their pound of flesh at their free will. The leading citizens of the city approached Maharaja Ranjit Singh to take over the city and restore order, which he did without much persuasion.

Emperor Bahadur Shah now appreciated the gravity of the situation and made a bee-line to Punjab without halting at Delhi on his way back from fighting the Rajputs. He ordered general mobilization and declared "jihād" (holy war) against the Sikhs. The far superior forces of the Mughals' lost no time in re-establishing the Mughal rule. The Emperor was again in control of the Malwa region by December 1710 while Banda and his force had retreated to the hills, pursued and persecuted by the combined armies of Mughals, Meos, Pathans, Afghans and the Rajputs. However, they did not succeed in capturing Banda Bahadur. Meanwhile, the Emperor died, perhaps over his failure to catch the big fish, once again leading to the usual fratricidal war of succession. Once that was settled attention was again riveted on Banda Bahadur who was besieged in the hills along with his small band of faithful followers. After eight long months of siege the Sikh force was starved into surrender on December 17, 1715 and prisoners were marched to Delhi where they were tortured to no end. Finally, the executions commenced in March 1716 and carried on *ad infinitum* for months together as if it was a '*tamasha*', an entertainment feature for the public of Delhi in which seven hundred Sikhs were publicly executed. These gory proceedings went on for almost three months culminating on June 19, 1716 in the execution of Banda Bahadur, his four-year old son, five of his commanders and a small band of loyal followers, thus bringing to an end an episode of unparalleled bravery, endurance and military prowess rarely found in the annals of military history.

Guru Granth Sahib

6

Scriptures and their recitation form part of every religion of the world. There is hardly any religion that does not have its sacred scriptures, be it Bhagavad Gītā and scores of other Hindu scriptures, the Bible for the Christians, the Kôra'n for the Muslim, and so on. But Sikhism is the only religion which accords the highest respect and importance to their sacred scripture, the Guru Granth Sahib. No prayer or function is even started, let alone completed without the ceremonial installation of Guru Granth Sahib. In fact, a function or ceremony of whatever nature can begin only after installation of the sacred Guru Granth Sahib. Its carriage from one place to another also requires special procedure and ceremony. Putting it to bed at night and installing it in the morning also require proper ceremony. Further, at the end of every session or termination of a function it is mandatory to recite the Sikh prayer called *Ardās*, which is recited in unison. The *Ardās* has three parts. The middle portion is a sort of remembrance of trials and triumphs through which the Sikh Panth has gone through. It is a sort of homage. Here it should be noted that Guru Granth Sahib did not exist during the time of Guru Nanak while the Vedas, Bible and the holy Kôra'n were very much part of the religious life of the communities concerned. Meanwhile, the holy-scripture **Adi Granth,** Guru Granth Sahib, was formally compiled by the Fifth Nanak, Guru Arjan Dev (1536-1606; Guruship 1581-1606). No doubt, the Holy Scripture had been composed from time to time by the preceding Gurus and many other important persons, the credit for its formal compilation, arrangement of verses according to *Ragas* or musical measure, go to the Fifth Guru. The hymns of First Nanak came first as *Mohalla* I (read as *Mohalla Pehla*) then came those of the Second Nanak as Guru-*Mohalla* II and so on. The *Bani* of the Gurus was followed by verses of other Indian saints,

Hindus and Muslims. In this way the hymns of the Adi Granth were set according to thirty-one Indian Classical Ragas.

There was no distinction of Hindu or Muslim, rich or poor, high caste or low caste in the Adi Granth. The Fifth Nanak, Guru Arjan Dev, thus created an ocean of Holy Scripture. It was called "Adi Granth" and by virtue of its universal character, it was certainly "not a bible for the Sikhs alone", nor was it a life history of the Sikh Gurus; in fact, it contains Universal Truth each and every word of which is dedicated to the Glory of the Almighty God only. The *Adi Granth* was completed in 1604 A.D. and installed by Guru Ram Das the same year in Hari Mandir, later called the Golden Temple, in a village initially known as Guru ka Chak renamed as Ramdaspur and eventually to be the exalted city of Amritsar. Bhai Buddha was appointed as the first *Granthi* (priest) of the highest seat of Sikh religion. Besides the Golden Temple there are many other sacred pilgrimage centers where the Sikhs pay their homage. One of the most important such shrine is Hemkund Sahib, located in Garhwal Himalayas at an altitude of about 15,000 feet. It is believed that Guru Gobind Singh meditated at this place during an earlier birth.[1]

No doubt the Adi Granth was compiled by Guru Arjan but the initiative in collecting the hymns of Farid, Kabir, *et al*, was Guru Nanak's. The *Bhagat Bani* of Adi Granth as it is called contains compositions by twelve non-Sikhs – two Muslims, Farid and Kabir, and the rest were Hindus. Obviously, the Bhagat Bani already existed when the Adi Granth was compiled to which Kabir's contribution is 541 hymns[2], mostly without comment or modification while those by Farid are liberally edited. The inclusion of compositions by non-Sikhs added to the catholicity of the Sikh Panth so as to make it popular and acceptable as widely as possible besides throwing new light on Guru Nanak's concept of *Gurbani*.

The cruel and torturous execution of the Fifth Guru Arjan aroused all-round revulsion and mass hysteria. It led to the establishment of "*Akāl Takhat*" (Timeless Throne) in 1606. Over

1. *The Indian Express*, North American Edition dated February 24, 2006; p. 46.
2. Kabir had acquired a reputation of being a pungent enunciator of simple rustic truths.

the centuries millions of innocent Hindu men, women and children were mercilessly put to the sword by the invading savages and their new convertees, all because of religious bigotry. With the installation of Adi Granth and Akāl Takhat, a new spirit of self-defense and fight for righteousness grew amongst the populace. A period of 239 years was to elapse between the First and the Tenth Nanak, the ten Gurus, during which Sikhism developed its philosophy and congregational methodology besides symbols and forms as well as creating a military force to wage war against Mughal rulers' atrocities.

Yet another significant function of Guru Nanak's movement was that he made normal household life as an essential pre-requisite for mystic training, which by itself was contrary to prevailing practice amongst various religions and sects. He declared himself positively in favor of worldly life, in accepting duties, obligations and responsibilities of an average human individual. Enforcement of differential symbolic features designed to make all Sikhs look distinctly different from Hindus and Muslims was yet another profound development. The Five K's and the Khanda added major symbolism, besides some others.[3]

The Khanda: This insignia of Sikhism is a synthesis of three symbols. The central symbol is the Khanda, a vertical double edged sword with a broad blade which represents the creative power of God. It exercises control over life and death of all beings. The right edge of the double-edged sword symbolizes freedom and authority embodied in moral and spiritual values while the left edge represents Divine Justice. On the left side of the emblem is a curved sword signifying "spiritual sovereignty" called *Piri* and on the right side is a similar curved sword known as *Miri*, symbolizing "Political Sovereignty". Inside the emblem is a steel-ring called Chakra[4] representing the Unity of God, the whole symbolizes all embracing divine manifestation, without beginning or end, neither first nor last, timeless and absolute, symbolizing God's concern for Truth, Justice and His spiritual power.

---

3. The Five K's: *Kesa; Kangha; Kachha; Kara; Kirpan.*
4. In the eighteenth century the Chakra was used as weapon of war. It was worn around the turban by all Sikh warriors.

Systematic persecution of Hindus by Muslim rulers attracted more and more persons to the cult of the Gurus thereby swelling their ranks many fold. At present the Sikhs number about twenty-three million, most live in Punjab. However, there is hardly any corner on planet earth where one would not find a Sikh, they being a highly enterprising community. About half a million Sikhs live in North America and another about 150,000 live in Canada. The dispute about furniture in the langars (community kitchens/dining halls), particularly in Canada has led to lot of bad blood but that does not concern this work. Anyway the matter has since been more or less resolved.

Transcendent & Immanent: God is the Creator. The Universe is his creation, but it is not part of Him. He is distinct from His Creation. The Universe is in time and space while God is limitless, not bound by time or space. He is in the Universe, but still out of it. He is transcendent, Eternal and Self-existent, beyond description and comprehension. In Hinduism and Sikhism, God is both transcendent and immanent. In Islam God is supposed to be only transcendent although the immanent aspect of God is accepted by implication. On the other hand in Christianity the immanent aspect of God is clearly accepted and emphasized while His Transcendence goes without saying. Above all, God does not incarnate; He is self-existent and formless. Since God is pervading everywhere, He is Immanent; and yet He is beyond everything, beyond pleasure and pain, and thus He is transcendent. "Every thing that God created is potentially holy, and our task as humans is to find that holiness in seemingly unholy situations. When we can do this, we will have learned to nurture our souls."

Nām

7

Sikh theology has imparted a specific significant meaning to the simple sounding term 'Nām'. Even Sikhism is often called 'Nām Marg' – the way or path as indicated and amplified by Nām. Sikhism believes that Nām is the Creator of everything. It sustains all regions and universe, all thought, knowledge and consciousness. Nām gives form to everything and through Nām comes Wisdom or Light. He who imbibes Nām reaches the highest state of development. Nām is '*Amrit*', the Nectar and it permeates the body and everything else. It is immaculate, is unfathomable and is within us. The question naturally arises: What is the difference between God and Nām? God and Nām are one and the same: "Nām is the Creative and Dynamic Immanence of God, the Reality sustaining, working and directing the manifest world of force and form.... The Self-Existent God manifested himself into Nām." Then came the creation of the universe. He permeates it, and reveals Himself in His creation.

According to Hindu-Sikh beliefs, there are 2.5 million forms of life of which the Human form is the highest and most precious gift. It is indeed a lucky soul that gets birth, or rebirth, in human form thus getting an opportunity to seek unity with the supreme-being. As opposed to the Hindu concept of seeking paradise, or *Swarg*, as the ultimate goal of human life, "the ultimate goal of Sikh religion is to merge with the Supreme Soul and then enjoy the Uninterrupted Bliss for ever". Without saying so in so many words, Sikhism aims at what Buddhism, as well as Tibeto-Buddhism, lays down the goal of human endeavor in this world i.e., "Nirvana" – release from the cycle of birth and death. It is a state of spiritual union with the Universal Soul which encompasses all beings. That blissful state is the ultimate goal from which the individual soul never returns, but remains merged in the ultimate Consciousness for ever and ever.

Tibeto-Buddhism differs drastically, indeed radically, from other religions including Sikhism in as much as it does not believe in one sole Creator of the universe. On the other hand, Sikhism, like most other religions, believes that there is but One God, who is both Impersonal (*Nirgun*) and Personal (*Sargun*). God is infinite. While Infinite can manifest itself into unlimited number of finite forms, but the sum of all the finite forms cannot add up to the Infinite. While the theory of Karma and Transmigration of Soul is common to all, the concept of **Nām** (Divine Name) appears to be exclusive to Sikhism. In Sikh Faith it is *Vāk* – the goddess of speech of the Vedas. However, it merely appears to be so since ramifications of **NĀM** are also as universal as man's perception of God Almighty. Both are one and the same thing; one is an aspect of the other – formless, infinite, colorless, markless, shapeless and eternal, sustaining and controlling all beings, each one in its entirety – body, speech and mind. The devotees may call God by various names but the foremost name of God as depicted in Sikhism is 'SAT', the Eternal Truth. Moreover, NĀM is a mystic word; in Sikh religion this mystic word is called "***Waheguru***" meaning Wonderful God, or 'Thou art Wonderful'. Meditation, contemplation and repetition of God, by whatever name, adds to His presence in our Consciousness. Congregational rendering of NĀM in musical format makes it easier to invoke one's consciousness to the maximum level into the presence of God. That is the crux of religious practice that ultimately leads a person to eternal bliss. The Hare Krishna movement in the West, the USA in particular, their deep concentration and single minded repetition of *bhakti-bhajan* accompanied by various musical instruments, carries them over to a state of mind merged in contemplation of the God Almighty, by whatever name or means it may be.

Prayer and Praise in the name of God, NĀM, rids the mind of evil thoughts and impurities leading to a glorious transformation in the human Soul and Mind ultimately imparting **Absolute Bliss**. Just as happiness is a state of mind, so is Absolute Bliss:

> "His soul and body dyed with the Name of One God
> Shall ever abide with the Supreme Soul.

As water blendeth with water,
So light is blended with Light.
Transmigration is ended and rest obtained–
Nanak is ever a sacrifice to the Lord."

(Gauri Sukhmani Mohalla 5: 11-8)

The material needs of the human body are essential pre-requisites to fulfil life functions. The question arises: how much? While it is primarily a function of personal equation, the individual has to draw the line between luxury and necessity. Again, what may be a bare necessity for one might be construed as luxury by another. The social and economic norms of the community should be taken as the guidelines:

"As a lotus flower remains unaffected in water
As also a duck swims in it and is not drenched by water
So with fixed intent on Sabad realizing NĀM
Oh Nanak, the dreadful world ocean is crossed safely."

The Concept of *Haumain*: English language, like any other for that matter, has its limitations in as much as many Asian concepts cannot be accurately translated, while for some others we just cannot find English words. When the concept does not exist in the mind, obviously, there cannot be a vocal expression for it. In this case 'Ego' would be the nearest in meaning. Haumain is the "I" of the normal human psyche. It is the conscious subject and directs the functioning of all our organs and limbs including the nervous system. It is the God created individual-self, or *Haumain*, which was essential for the growth of individual life. It has five principal classes of vices: Lust (*Kām*); Anger (*Karodh*); Greed and covetousness (*Lobh*); Attachment (*Moh*) and Pride (*Ahankar*). *Haumain* amounts to self-centeredness; it must be substituted by God-centeredness – *Manmukh* (self-centered) to be replaced by *Gurmukh* (God-centered).

The Doctrine of Karma: There is a certain difference of opinion whether this Doctrine is accepted in Sikhism or not. While in general terms it seems to be accepted, it is rejected in its fatalistic or deterministic sense. Guru Granth Sahib states: "Lord created the world and left it free to do as it wills." God created man and granted him freedom to decide the course of his life. "According to their deeds, some are near and some are far from God.... Man is blessed with the light of reason and discrimination.... Vices are like chains around our necks and virtues are the only friends." If man was to be rigidly governed by his previous deeds, if his present and future actions were to be predetermined by his deeds in his past life, or even the present one for that matter, the question of his having the freedom to shape his life does not arise. Evidently, the Gurus do not accept the validity of any Karmic or deterministic law. Islam and Christianity too hold similar views since God's Will alone prevails, and not the actions of the man – good, bad or indifferent. Moral life is fundamental tenet of Sikhism.

Sarbat Khālsā

8

After Guru Gobind Singh left this mortal world the Sikhs did not have a personal leader to resolve day-to-day matters of the community. A tradition of settling various issues through consensus at community meetings came into being, perhaps more by accident than by deliberation. The meetings were held at Amritsar, at Akāl Takhat or Darbar Sahib, and in course of time it became SOP (Standard Operating Procedure) to hold these assemblies biennially on the first of *Baisākh* and on the festive occasion of *Deepavali, Diwali* in Punjab. The resolutions passed in these assemblies were mandatory and came to be accorded the status of *Gurmatā*, Decree of the Guru. This procedure did have teething troubles by way of differences amongst various factions but these internal squabbles were soon settled one way or the other after which the Sarbat Khālsā became a powerful institution in its own right.

A number of *jathedārs* had been appointed by Sarbat Khālsā and allocated various duties. Many jathedārs acquired a small number of horsemen and operated independently according to their whims and fancies. There was no central control over these roving bands of cavalry-men. When it appeared that matters might get out of hand, the Sarbat Khālsā held on October 14, 1745, Diwali of 1745, passed a *Gurmatā* ordering merger of all horsed-*jathās* to be reorganized into twenty-five cavalry regiments under command of Nawab Kapur Singh as the overall commander of the Sikh Army. An unfortunate episode arising through some misdemeanor of some cavalry men resulted in terrible retribution on the Sikhs. About seven thousand Sikhs were killed in a totally unequal fight and another three thousand were made prisoners. They were taken to Lahore and executed at Shahidganj. This terrible disaster of June 1746 has come be known as the *Ghallūghārā*, the holocaust[1].

The Sikh Army Commander, Nawab Kapur Singh was getting old. Therefore, in another Sarbat Khālsā the Sikh Army, the *Dal* Khālsā, was divided into eleven *misls* under overall command of Jassa Singh while Nawab Kapur Singh remained the nominal Supreme Commander. All *misls* were nominally equal but in fact they varied considerably in their fighting strength and influence so much so that some *misls* had a few hundred soldiers, while others had more than ten thousand battle worthy troops. It is estimated that the Dal Khālsā had the capacity to put in the field at one time about seventy thousand horse and foot soldiers.

1. Khushwant Singh: *A History of the Sikhs*, vol. I; Oxford University Press, New Delhi; 1999/2006.

Nanak "Lama": The Tibetan Connection

9

In the words of His Holiness the Dalai Lama: "Guru Nanak, due to his unique lifestyle, is the brightest star among most brilliant ones in the sky." In fact, most of the Tibetans consider Guru Nanak as their guardian deity and protector. They worship him and call him **Nanak Lama**. This is their way of showing respect, devotion and honoring a godly person. Not only that, a large number of Tibetans consider Guru Nanak as **reincarnation of Padmasambhava** – an important Lama of Indian origin. Not only that, they claim that in times of their distress "Nanak Lama" has always come to their rescue. And that is not all. Statues of Guru Nanak are found installed in a number of Buddhist temples in Ladakh (then part of Tibet), and Tibet, especially in the Tibetan temples of Lake Mansarovar, Chamoli valley, etc. Guru Nanak's itinerary in Ladakh also included Chasūl-Upashi-Karu. On the southeast of Karu there are two villages whose inhabitants worship only Guru Nanak, and no other gods or goddesses.

Once while traveling through Tibet, Baba Nanak and his party including many Tibetans ran short of water. It was a distressing situation. However, "Nanak Lama" placed his rosary on the surface of the nearby frozen lake which melted into sweet water in a matter of moments. Since then butter-lamps are lighted regularly to worship Nanak Rinpoché. Yet another incident during Nanak Lama's travels through Tibetan territory established his reputation as a man of God possessing supernatural powers. During late 1970's **Leh-Nima Road** was under construction by the Border Roads Organization of India. A huge boulder was found blocking the trace-cut on the proposed alignment. The dozer operator tried to move the boulder but in vain. In fact, the dozer-blade was severely damaged while he attempted to clear the boulder. By that time it was late evening and the work was called off. At night the operator dreamt that he must not move that boulder, and let it lie where it was. Next morning the operator narrated his dream to his officer, a military man who dismissed the idea out of hand. But the dozer did not succeed in moving the boulder out of the way. It was, therefore, decided to demolish the big boulder by explosive-charge. Next day happened to be a Sunday and hence no road work. It was then that a number of Tibetans were seen lighting butter-lamps and worshipping before the big boulder. On enquiry, the Tibetans informed the army officer that it was not a stone but a wax-statute of their revered Baba Nanak Lama on which the Guru's torso – head, shoulder and back – were imprinted.

Through further enquiries it was established that during the period 1515-1518 A.D. when Baba Nanak was returning to Punjab via Kashmir after his tour of Sikkim, Nepal and Tibet, Baba Nanak rested at that spot for a day. The legend has it that an old woman came to Nanak Lama and narrated her story of a demon who had to be fed a human body everyday to placate him, and that the next day was the turn of her son to be presented to the demon as his meal. Baba Nanak advised the woman not to send her son to the demon at the appointed time and place, which in turn made the demon very angry. The Demon took vengeance by sliding a large boulder down the hill towards Baba Nanak to crush him. But the boulder did not crush Nanak Lama, and instead it just touched him, stopped where the Lama was meditating, and turned into wax with an imprint of the Lama. The Demon was thus subdued. In turn the Border Roads detachment thanked their stars that they did not demolish the Boulder. Instead, a beautiful Gurudwara known as ***Pather Sahib*** was built in memory of Guru Nanak, about twenty-five miles away from Leh on Leh-Kargil road at an altitude of about 12,000 ft.*** Tibetan Buddhists often worship at this Gurudwara. No wonder, therefore, that the adventurous spirit of the Sikhs has taken them to every nook and corner of the world.

In a lighter vein a joke making the rounds in Northern India goes something like this: When Tenzing Norgay (and Edmund Hillary) climbed the 8,848 meters (29,028 feet ASL) Mount Everest (Sagarmatha in Nepalese and Chomolungma in Tibetan/ Sherpa) on May 29, 1953, Tenzing boasted that he was the first human being to set foot on the highest mountain on Planet Earth.

***Photos by kind courtesy of Colonel S.S. Kahlon, Commander 16 Border Roads Task Force, GREF.

Same instant, a Sikh appeared as if from nowhere and said: "Sherji! You must be tired. Please have this cup of tea!..."[1]

Thyangboche Monastery is situated at the base of Mount Everest in the village of Solo Khumbu. The leader of the 1964-Indian Everest Expedition visited this Monastery. He was shown a number of sacred text and idols one of which was that of Guru Rinpoché, the name by which the Tibetans remember Guru Nanak.

Tibetan reverence for Guru Nanak is personally confirmed by Colonel Nirmal Singh, a Mountain Gunner who has written to me:

> I was on a reconnaissance mission in North Sikkim during April 1963. In Tibet Sikkim is known as Den-jong, or the "rice country". We were at the base of the 18,000 feet Yaka-la, when I saw a large number of local Lamas sitting in rows and reciting something that was totally unintelligible to me. On enquiry it was revealed that they were celebrating Guru Nanak's Birthday!

The date of birth of Guru Nanak has been a subject of controversy amongst Sikh intelligentsia. Baba Sandhu in his Janamsakhi has recorded that Baba Nanak was born on Kartik Pûranmâshi, Full Moon day in end October-early November. But Bala Janamsakhi is generally considered spurious. Nonetheless, Guru Nanak's birthday continues to be officially observed on Full Moon day in the month of Kartik as a matter of continuation of tradition and convenience. However, Bhai Mân Singh has argued in favor of Baisakh Pûranmâshi as the correct birthday of the Guru. Taking all facts into cinsideration the latter version is found to be factually correct. There is no doubt that Baba Nanak was born on Pûranmâshi day in Sambat 1526 of Indian calendar in the month of Baisakh on the third day of the first quarter of the moon in the early hours of the dawn, three hours before sunrise, corresponding to 15 April 1469.

Obviously, even more than five hundred years ago the Tibetans knew the correct date of birth of Guru Nanak while most Indian Hindus and Sikhs were ignorant of the factual position. Indeed, they were celebrating Guru Nanak's birth anniversary on the historically correct date when Colonel Nirmal Singh happend to pass by their congregation!

---

1. Contributed by Colonel Nirmal Singh.

The Boulder that added a page to Sikh history and gave the characteristic name to the Gurudwara **"PATHER SAHIB"**

Gurudwara Pather Sahib
A landmark in the lap of the snowbound Himalayas

A place of worship in pristine environment

A sacred structure built in the clouds

A replica of the Boulder created indoors in
everlasting memory of Baba Nanak
(Original painting by S. Shobha Singh)

The Sanctum Sanctorum in the Frozen Land

The Tapo Asthan

Baba Nanak in Baghdad

10

Within hours of landing in Baghdad in July 1982, my first thoughts were of the central Graveyard of that ancient historical city. Why a Cemetery of all the places! – Sikh Faith was, and still is our Family Religion, as it was of a large number of Punjabi and Sindhi Hindu migrants from West Punjab-Sindh, Pakistan. During my childhood my Grandmother had told us a number of stories one of which was about the visit of Baba Nanak to Baghdad besides Mecca and Medina. A number of Sikh *Sangats* had talked about a Samadhi of Guru Nanak in Baghdad which was reported to be in a rather lonely corner of a graveyard in Baghdad. So I made enquiries from an odd Sikh that I met in the city, but they thought I had gone nuts asking such stupid questions. The younger generation of Sikhs was not privy to such lesser-known truths about Sikhism, and at that time in Baghdad they were more concerned with the Iraq-Iran War that was raging in full ferocity rather than about when, where and how Guru Nanak had been to Baghdad, if at all.

While familiarizing myself with this exotic City, I was walking around the outskirts in search of the graveyard of my old memories when an Arab family man at a distance shouted on top of his voice: "Sat Sri Akaal"! I was completely taken aback. We met, shook hands, but he would not answer my questions; instead he insisted on inviting me to his house. I feigned reluctance, but was easily persuaded to accept the invitation. He was originally a Punjabi Sikh, now a clean shaven man with no pretence to Sikhism. He had stayed back in Iraq after the Second World War, married a local beauty and raised a family. That is nothing to get surprised at since Iraqi women have well cut features, are fair and generally beautiful, with the exception of those who are heavy weight champions. He had become an Iraqi in and out, and spoke the local dialect fluently.

After the usual obligatory refreshments he gave me directions to the central cemetery. Since it was already sun-down, there was no question of our going to the place that evening. His offer of taking me to the place next day after his day's work was most tempting, but I had very little time in Baghdad and so politely declined the offer. In any case mine was a sort of personal pilgrimage. I wanted to be left alone with my thoughts and memories of my childhood spent in a predominantly Muslim village where the only source of early education, KG so to say, was in a masjid under a staunch Mullah who did not miss any opportunity to abuse the Hindus at the slightest provocation. And he addressed children like me as "*Karar*[1] *da Puttar*"!

In those days the Indian Government permitted a maximum of twenty US dollars to foreign travelers like me, but fortunately I had a couple of hundred left over from my previous work-stay in Yemen. I could, therefore, be on my own to pursue my search.

A taxi dropped me at the outskirts of the Cemetery. The driver just would not take me any further nor talk about the subject on my mind although I had a smattering of Arabic speech. While roaming around in the secluded desolate place I spotted a small single storey house-like structure and made a bee-line to the place. Lo and behold! That is precisely what I was looking for. It was a small mosque, just a two-room set. As soon as one entered the place one was face to face with the grave of a Muslim saint. Incidentally, Shia Muslims believe in saints and 'Pīrs' and treat their graves with a sort of veneration. At the end of the entrance-passage there was another low door-way leading to another room. And that indeed proved to be a surprise of a lifetime! It was just like what used to be a common practice in our village we had left in Pakistan. A gurudwara and a mandir in the same building-complex with a common entrance...if you were a Hindu, you first went to the mandir part of the building and then to the gurudwara; and if you were a Sikh, it was *vice versa*. It was as if I was living through my childhood at the ripe old age of past fifty. It was the same story here in the vast graveyard in Baghdad where not a soul – a living

1. *Karar*: A derogatory term reserved for Hindus in erstwhile West Punjab (Pakistan). And 'Puttar' means son.

soul of flesh and blood I mean – was to be seen. However, the inner low door led to what for all practical purposes was a gurudwara, with a Samadhi of Baba Nanak and a big painting of the Saint in the dark dingy background.

The Mullah in charge of the premises found it infra-dig to converse with me, but he did mention that the place I had just been belonged to **"Nanak Pīr"** or **"Wali-Hind Baba Nanak"** – the title by which Guru Nanak is known in Afghanistan too, or at least what was so till the Russian Communism, the notorious Taliban and the worthy Yankees played merry havoc with the country. It left me in no doubt that Baba Nanak used to be a venerated 'Pīr' of Baghdad, besides many other parts of the Middle East.

Baghdad is an Iranian word which literally means "a gift given by God". The old city of Baghdad used to be situated on the western bank of river Euphrates. After the old city got ruined, the new habitation came up on the eastern bank, and that is where Guru Nanak visited the place. When the Guru and his '*chela*' Mardānā reached Baghdad, they found a place to stay behind the present railway station located on the western bank of the river. It is connected to the new city by a bridge. As usual the duo woke up early and started singing hymns (kīrtan in Sikh terminology). Some people objected to this since singing was taboo in Islam.

The place where Guru Nanak and Bhai Mardānā stayed in west of Baghdad lies between the old graveyard to the north and the present Baghdad-Samra rail line to the south. Here used to be a simple raised platform, about 4 × 3 feet and about 3-4 feet high, on which Guru Nanak used to sit. The courtyard in front of the room had a boundary wall on which there was an inscription in Arabic. It was dated 927 Hijri which roughly corresponds to 1520 CE. It is well on the cards that those relics no longer exist as such. However, the *Subis* people (*Al Sabia* or *Sabian*) used to live in Iraq till about sixties of the 20th Century. They were natives of Southern Iraq and used to wear long unshorn hair and beard. They were staunch followers of Guru Nanak and used to wear Guru Nanak's portrait around their necks. Neither they called themselves Muslims nor did the other Iraqis recognized them as Muslims. They merely called themselves followers of Guru Nanak.

11 Guru Nanak: From Middle East Back to India

Bhai Gurdas has mentioned in his first Vār the often talked about miracle that is claimed to have occurred during Guru Nanak's visit to Mecca. He was wearing the obligatory blue garments, had a staff in his hand and the holy Kôra'n in his armpit. A *kūzā* (cup for ablutions) and a prayer mat were the other obligatory items to be carried by a *hāji*. At night the Guru fell asleep with his feet towards *Mihrāb* – the niche in the center of the wall facing Mecca. The keeper of the premises hit Guru Nanak with his leg and admonished him for stretching his feet towards the House of God. He got hold of his legs and turned him around. As he did so, even Mecca revolved along with the Guru causing all round amazement. All bowed before Guru Nanak (*Pauri* 32). Another similar story is related to Guru's visit to Medina where his reputation had spread in advance of his arrival. On arrival at Medina the Guru asked Bhai Mardānā to play on his *rebeck** and sing one of his favorite hymns. As he did so, the congregation came forward with stones in their hands to stone the visitors to death for the sacrilege of singing in the sacred premises. However, the Muslims could not throw their stones which remained stuck to their hands. Instead, they all bowed before the Saint. The stones got unstuck and fell off the hands of the people after Imam Jafar, the descendant of Hazrat Ali, interceded on their behalf. A house in memory of Nanak Pīr stands about five km from the burial place of the Prophet.

The triumphs of Guru Nanak in Mecca, Medina and Baghdad are popular subjects of *Janamsakhis*. Since *Janamsakhis* are essentially hagiographic, their version cannot be taken on face value. However, the fact of Guru's travels to far off lands cannot be disputed. The Author has personally visited the mosque-cum-gurudwara structure in the midst of a graveyard in Baghdad; the Sikh temple is a memorial to Guru's visit to Baghdad. Prayers and worship in the Gurudwara was

---

* Rebeck (also spelt as rebec) is a medieval three-stringed musical instrument, an early form of 'fiddle' and called rabâb in Arabic.

done on a regular basis with suitable adjustment of time-schedules. The significant point is that both the Darbar Sahib and the mosque were, and perhaps still are under one roof. Furthermore, Tibetans are not the only non-Indians who look up to Guru Nanak with reverence. The Guru is known as **"Nanak Buddha"** in Sri Lanka, **'Wali-Hind Baba Nanak'** in Afghanistan, **'Nanak Pīr'**, **'Pīr Baba Nanak'**, or **'Bal Gundari'** in what is now called Middle East, while he was referred to as **"Bhusa Nanak"** in Vietnam, Mongolia and parts of China. "No other prophet could get such universal respect, recognition, and reverence during his own lifetime as was received by Guru Nanak."

When Guru Nanak left Baghdad after a stay of nearly four months, a *Chola* (cloak) was presented to him with verses from the Holy Kôra'n embroidered on it. This *Chola* is preserved at Dera Baba Nanak (DBN).

It would be of interest to mention that Guru Nanak made it a point to visit Jerusalem to meet with the leading lights of Judaism and Christianity, and held discussions with them as he had done with various Muslim theologians. And did Guru Nanak visit Africa? Perhaps he did. Sudan and Abyssinia are specifically mentioned in this context since Guru Nanak was severely persecuted in the latter country. Moreover, it is reported that near Kampala there is a village named Bab Nanika, so named perhaps in honor of Guru Nanak. Janamsakhis report that on his return from Sudan Guru Nanak paid a short visit to Damascus-Allepo region where a mosque in honor of Wali Hind was built near that of Baba Farīd. It seems Syria to Istanbul in Turkey was just a hop away. However, there is no evidence or indirect reference to Guru's sojourn to the seat of Roman Catholicism, the Vatican. However, there are certain indications that Guru Nanak might have made a brief halt in Azerbaijan where some tablets inscribed with Mūl Mantra in Gurmukhi script have been found.

Persia, Persian language and Persian invasions have had a profound effect on the cultural and religious traditions of India. So Guru Nanak did make it a point to visit Tehran. The Guru next visited Uzbekistan where some people took to reciting *Japji* in their own language daily, while in another town they were staunch followers of Guru Nanak Wali Hind. The great cultural center of Central Asia, Samarkand was the next stop. On his way back home Guru Nanak met Babur at Kabul. His visit to the great trading center of Balkh (modern Wazirabad) is still remembered when five handfuls of rice fed the entire congregation at Pīr Balāgh Dān and the pot got empty only when the Guru left the place. To take the story a step further: When Babur invaded India Guru Nanak and many other faqirs were arrested. They were ordered to grind corn for his armies. The Guru's grindstone kept working automatically while Nanak moved around freely. The incident was reported to Babur. He recognized Guru Nanak, sought his pardon and ordered his release; but the Guru insisted on all faqirs to be released which Babur did. The two pieces of grindstone are still preserved as memorable relics.

Bhai Mardānā had died in Afghanistan. Guru Nanak then left Afghanistan via Khyber Pass, reached Peshawar. He crossed River Sind (Attock) and reached Hassan Abdāl, the site of the famous shrine of Panjā Sahib whose background history follows more or less a similar pattern as of Gurudwara Pather Sahib – Hassan Abdāl was the seat of a mystic saint known as Vali Kandhāri, or the mystic from Kandhār, a person proud of his position and occult powers. Guru Nanak's companion felt very thirsty and the Guru advised him to go up the hill and get some water from the mystic to quench his thirst. He climbed the hill all the way up and requested Vali Kandhāri for some drinking water; but he was rudely told to return to his Hindu Saint and tell him to use his occult powers, if at all he has any, and get some water for his thirsty infidel companion. The matter was reported to the Guru who, after thinking for a moment, told his followers to dig up the earth. As soon as a big boulder was moved aside, fresh sparkling water gushed out. Vali Kandhāri was terribly upset. In a fit of jealousy he threw a huge boulder towards them. The Guru halted the big boulder with the palm of his right hand. The boulder stopped there and then with an imprint of the Guru's palm on it. In course of time this spring was further developed and a beautiful Gurudwara built at the site. It is still there and during pre-partition days the Author had personally visited the shrine a few times and saw for himself the boulder with the imprint of a palm. A great fair is held at the Shrine on Baisākhi day.

Significance of Guruship

12

The word 'Guru' has a special significance in Sikhism. It is not merely a 'teacher' or guide or an expert; far from it. Here 'GU' means darkness and 'RU' means Light: Thus, 'Guru' means light that dispels all darkness and is called 'JOT' or Divine Light. Hence when Impersonal God manifested his attributes in person, that person was called Guru Nanak. In short, Guru Nanak was the embodiment of Divine Light. That is only part of the explanation since the word Guru is used in three inter-related aspects:

Firstly:

Guru stands for God Almighty, the All-Pervading Divine Spirit, and the Divine Light;

"The Guru is Beneficent, the Sanctuary of peace,
The Guru is the Light of three Worlds,
He is the Eternal Being,
Oh Nanak, he who believeth in Him, attaineth peace."

(Slok Mohalla 1; p. 137)

The Guru is All-Powerful,
The Guru is the Formless Lord,
The Guru is the Highest, Fathomless and Limitless,
Ineffable is His Praise; what can a sayer say?

(Kanra Mohalla 4; p. 1310)

The Guru is Infinite God Himself,
Nanak, meditate on such a Guru day and night.

(Sri Rag Mohalla 5; p. 53)

Secondly:

The prefix 'Guru' is also used for Guru Nanak as he was the Embodiment of God's Light.

"Guru Nanak is the perfect Guru,
With the true Guru I meditateth upon God."

(Nat Mohalla 4; p. 982)

"Guru Nanak is the true Guru,
The true Guru taketh me to God."
"The Guru and God are one,
Divine Master pervadeth everywhere."

(Ramkali Mohalla 4; p. 882)

Thirdly:

The word Guru is used for Gurbani also, the Divine Word. Since Gurbani came direct from God, and as there is no difference between God and His order (Divine Word), Gurbani is Guru too.

"The Word is the Guru,
And the Guru is the Word,
The Guru's Word is life-giving Elixir,
Whosoever shall obey, what the Word commandeth,
Verily he shall get salvation."

(Kanra Mohalla 4; p. 1310)

"The Word is the True Guru, and the Guru is the Word,
And the Word revealeth the path of salvation."

Chronology of Sikh Gurus 13

The years noted below against the name of each Guru relate only to the period of his Guruship. It is noteworthy that all the Gurus were *Khatris*, high caste Hindus.

1.	Guru Nanak	1469-1539	NANAK I
2.	Guru Angad	1539-1552	NANAK II
3.	Guru Amar Das	1552-1574	NANAK III
4.	Guru Ram Das	1574-1581	NANAK IV
5.	Guru Arjan (Executed in 1606)	1581-1606	NANAK V
6.	Guru Hargobind (Son of NANAK V)	1606-1645	NANAK VI
7.	Guru Har Rai	1644-1661	NANAK VII
8.	Guru Harkrishan	1661-1664	NANAK VIII
9.	Guru Tegh Bahadur (Executed: 1675)	1664-1675	NANAK IX
10.	Guru Gobind Singh	1675-1708	NANAK X

With the sole exception of Nanak II all subsequent appointments were hereditary. Guru Arjan, younger son of Guru Ram Das was the first of the Sikh Gurus to be born in a Sikh family. His father died when he was barely twenty years old. But he remembered that his grandfather, Nanak II had predicted that one day this young lad would lead the Panth. So he did. In fact, he proved to be the most energetic of all the Gurus with the possible exception of Nanak I and Nanak X. It was Nanak V who got the historic building constructed at Amritsar known as Hari Mandir or Darbar Sahib, later known as the famous Golden Temple. The initial building was destroyed three or four times in the eighteenth century. The present sacred structure dates from the time of Maharaja Ranjit Singh (1780-1839), the founder of the Sikh State in Punjab in 1801. The Sikh State was incorporated in the British Empire consequence of Sikh Wars (1845-1849). Before Ranjit Singh died in 1839 costly jewels were distributed to Brahmins so that a good place would be reserved for him in heaven. When he was cremated, four of his wives and seven concubines burnt themselves alive on his funeral pyre in the traditional Hindu custom of *sati*. It was sometime after this episode that the Kuka sect, Sahjdharis-Namdharis and the like came up as reform movements in Sikh religion. It would be of interest to point out that Ranjit Singh married twenty-two wives from whom he had seven sons. Besides these wives, he had numerous concubines too.

At this point of the narrative, episode of **Koh-i-Nūr**, the 'Mountain of Light', would be of historical interest. The Persian invader Nadir Shah having plundered and butchered the population of Mughal capital as well as Punjab was on his way back home in the summer of 1739. He took the easier route through Punjab following the low hills-tracks to avoid the heat of the plains. This was Dal Khalsa terrain. His caravan was laden with enormous booty which included the bejeweled peacock throne and the world famous diamond, Koh-i-Nūr, besides slaves in their thousands. The Khalsa had already set their eyes on the rich caravan, which they plundered *ad lib* throughout its passage through the Punjab. They preyed on the easy going triumphant caravan during the hours of darkness and before any body could react, they would disappear in the hills, never to be seen, and never to give conventional battle to the returning victorious invader.

After Nadir Shah's assassination his most trusted general, Ahmad Shah Abdali ascended the throne of Afghanistan, took possession of most of the looted treasure from India including the famous Diamond. The next owner of Koh-i-Nūr was Shah Zaman who in turn was blinded by his brother Mahmud. The bone of contention, the much coveted precious Diamond now fell in the hands of Afghan King Shah Shuja and his wife Wafa Begum. The wheel of fate took twists and turns and the Afghan royal family took shelter in Lahore under protection of Maharaja Ranjit Singh. Wafa Begum wanted her husband to join her at Lahore where he was ceremoniously received with honor. When the Begum continued to evade the issue of Koh-i-Nūr, Maharaja Ranjit Singh placed a heavy guard on the Afghan family besides putting them on reduced rations to the point of starvation. And that was it. The Afghans gave away the Diamond to the Maharaja on June 1, 1813.

Guru Arjan had to face the jealousy and animosity of his older brother Prithi Chand so much so that it gave rise to a rival sect known as '*minas*', a splinter group of Sikhs under Prithi Chand. Guru Arjan's only son was born in 1595, the future Nanak VI. The baby was named Hargobind, which means world-lord.[1] It was a matter of great joy, since hereditary succession was assured. The significance of this event lies in that the principle of hereditary succession was now established beyond any doubt. Although hereditary succession can lead to many complications like fratricidal wars amongst the Mughal princes, and so it did in the present case when two attempts were made by Prithi Chand to do away with Hargobind, the subsequent developments proved that this was a good augury for the Panth. Guru Gobind Singh (Nanak X) lost all four of his sons at the hands of Muslim executioners; that indeed was a major contributory factor in bringing the lineage to an end. The Mughal emperors' attempts at conversion of Sikhs (and Hindus) to Islam were so drastic and ruthless that "Had there been no Guru Gobind Singh, the entire country would have been converted to Islam."

The succession of Gurus, Nanak One to the Tenth was generally hereditary; personal suitability and acceptance by the congregation was also taken into consideration, since every subsequent Guru also became the embodiment of Divine Light as soon as Guruship was conferred on him. In this respect, the continuity of Nanak One to Nanak Ten varies from the Tibeto-Buddhist concept of continuity of Dalai Lama One to the Fourteenth. However, it was the Tenth Nanak, Guru Gobind Singh, who declared the end of succession to the *Gaddi* since all of his four sons had been sacrificed to the Panth. He instituted the sacred scripture, Sri Guru Granth Sahib, as the Guru *par excellence* thereby putting an end to any possible war of succession between

1. Both 'Hari' and 'Gobind' are popular names for Lord Vishnu.

the claimants to the highest seat of Sikh religion. Thus the "Eleventh Guru-to-be" was reduced to "Pretender to the Throne"; the "Nanak Jot", the Light Supreme, was passed on to Adi Granth, and the Holy Scripture was proclaimed the last and only Guru for ever thereafter. Nanak Ten did so by placing the Adi Granth on the throne of Nanak One together with five paise and a coconut and then bowed before it declaring it to be the last Guru for ever. In this manner when Guruship was passed on to Adi Granth, Guru Granth Sahib too became the embodiment of Divine Light. In other words, when Sikhs bow before Guru Granth Sahib, they are not worshipping or bowing before a mere Book; "they are doing so before the Divine Light or JOT (Guru) which was passed on when the Guruship was conferred upon it."

It is noteworthy that transformation from one Guru to the next took place in the same way as one lamp is lit from another. It was the same holy light carried through, the same "Divine Flame in continuity of the same Divine Mission", each one reincarnation of the previous one, from the beginning to the end, from the First Guru to the Tenth Guru. It is for this very sense of continuity of Divine Flame that, though all the ten Gurus carry individual names for purposes of identification, historically, they are designated as Nanak One, Nanak Two, Nanak Three, and so on to Nanak Ten. The analogy to Gyalwa Rinpoché, the Dalai Lama as One to Fourteen is much too obvious to require any elaboration. Similarly, as in Tibeto-Buddhism, in Sikhism too a man is called upon to "accept the Will of God and thus sublimate his suffering and loss" trusting in conquest of sorrow and suffering through ceaseless endeavor. However, the Sikh concept of reincarnation is vastly different from the Hindu or Buddhist system, even though essentially, all of them subscribe to the idea of incarnation in one form or the other. Obviously, the Eleventh Guru, Guru Granth Sahib is in a class by itself.

Sikh Scriptures

14

Nanak VII, Guru Har Rai, had excommunicated his son, Ram Rai, for the latter had tempered with the wording of Guru Granth Sahib. However, Emperor Aurangzeb was pleased with Ram Rai's performance and bestowed a tract of land near Dehradun as *jagir* on which the new sect built a gurudwara. Dehra is still the headquarters of the Sect.

Guru Nanak's eldest son Sri Chand was a celibate ascetic but the guru did not appoint him as his successor. He decided to break with the old Hindu ascetic tradition and appointed an unrelated devoted disciple, a simple family man as the next Guru. Sikhism thus broke with the ascetic tradition right from the start. Sikhs have been a body of householders ever since. 'Sikh' is a general term used to designate all followers of the ten Gurus. Although names of all Sikhs have the suffix 'Singh', strictly speaking, only those Sikhs who have received *amrit* (baptism) are entitled to the suffix Singh. However, at present this is merely a theoretical formality. The feminine counterpart of Singh is "*Kaur*" (Princess).

The decline of Moghul Empire gave the Sikhs an opportunity to create their confederacies, *misls*, eleven in number, each loosely organized under its local leader. That was the beginning of Sikh State in embryonic form.

Guru Arjan finished compilation of Adi Granth in 1604. There are two main editions of Adi Granth: one; written by Bhai Gur Das at Guru Arjan's dictation, and second; made by Guru Gobind Singh at Damdama Sahib in South Punjab by adding a small number of additional hymns and *Slokas* composed by Nanak IX (Guru Teg Bahadur). The Adi Granth opens with the *Mūl Mantra* (Root Verse) which may be freely translated as follows:

> There is but one God. If you care to name Him call Him Satya – one Who was, Who is, and Who shall be. He is the doer, all pervading, without fear, without enmity. His existence is unlimited by time. He is unborn, self-existent, and can be realized through the Grace of the Guru.

Since the *Mūl Mantra* contains the essence of Sikhism, the following alternative translation may be more acceptable:

> One God (OM) Whose name is Truth, Creator, without fear, without enmity, immortal, free from transmigration, self-existing; by the Guru's grace.

Nanak VIII to Nanak X had to face the ire of the Mughal Emperors to an exceptional degree of ferocity. The 8th Guru was a mere child of six and died at age nine to be followed by the Ninth Guru, Guru Tegh Bahadur (Guruship 1664-1675) who had a very troublesome life. He was very cruelly murdered by Aurangzeb and was succeeded by his son, the Tenth and the last Guru, Guru Gobind Singh who again was a mere boy. He was in mortal danger for his life after his Father's murder. Guru Gobind Singh spent the next about twenty years, more or less in hiding, in retirement, contemplating his life's mission and preparing for the pan-ultimate event in the history of Sikhism. Naturally he was bitter about the cruelties inflicted on his Father with the result that hatred for the Musalman became almost a duty for the son, indeed for the whole community. Eventually when he came out of retirement he was ready for the great mission of his life, determined to separate the Sikhs from men of all other faiths to avoid any confusion about identity. He called five devoted disciples and instituted a simple warrior-like ceremony of initiation, *Pahul*. He stirred some sweet water with his two edged '*kirpan*' (curved knife), and sprinkled the water thus made holy on the five disciples, the "*Panj Piyare*". He proclaimed them as "*Khalsa*", the pure ones, and added the epithet 'Singh', the Lion, after their names. The feminine counterpart of 'Singh' was introduced as 'Kaur', the Princess. The rule of 'Five-K's' came thereafter for all Sikhs to be observed as part of religious compulsion and distinction. Now onwards the Khalsa became separated, different from the Hindus. He proclaimed them all as the 'Khalsa', the pure ones, and added the epithet 'Singh' after their names. Going a step further, it was ordained that every "*ardās*", the supplicatory prayer, shall end with the words "*Raj Kare gā Khālsā*...":

> "The Khalsa shall rule
> Their enemies will be scattered.
> Only they that seek refuge will be saved."

The Imperial conquerors who entered India from the North-West in the eleventh century brought Islam to the subcontinent. They won many adherents, mostly through forced conversions. But it was through the Sufis – Muslim mystics and ascetics with pantheistic tendencies – that Islam entered the hearts of Hindus (and Sikhs).

Outstanding teachings of Sikhism are significant in themselves. The unique features of Sikhism are summarized below:

1. Possession of the original manuscript of scripture (Kartarpur Granth)
2. The Adi Granth as Guru of the Panth
3. The Langar, or free refectory for teaching equality
4. A succession of Ten Gurus embodying one Spirit
5. The Five Symbols
6. Guru Granth Sahib in a special script, Gurmukhi.

Sangat & Pangat

15

The *Langar* is a typically unique institution of the Sikh community. It plays a vital part in bringing the members of the community as well as outsiders to one level of social status – the ground level with the same food served to all irrespective of caste, creed, colour, sex or status. Sikhism is the only religion which welcomes each and everyone to its '*Langar*' (Free Community Kitchen) without any discrimination. Remember the tenets of Guru Nanak, his concepts of oneness of God and Universal Brotherhood of man? "If any community holds the key to national integration of India, it is the Sikhs all the way."

Nanak One introduced the institutions of *Sangat* and *Pangat* in the socio-religious set up of his disciples. He attached great importance to the concept and practice of congregation, as well as common community kitchens known as Langar. Sitting in assembly in single rows on the ground and eating the same food from the common free kitchen irrespective of caste, creed or status – that was the concept of Pangat. Although Sangat merely means congregation or assembly, amongst the Sikhs it is generally *Sat-Sangat* – the Holy Congregation. It has been defined by Nanak Four as:

> Sat-Sangat is the school of the True Guru,
> There we learn to love God and appreciate His greatness.
>
> (Var Kanra Mohalla 4; p. 1313)

The above institution of *Pangat* was so strictly followed that when Emperor Akbar and Raja of Haripur came to meet Nanak Three, Guru Amar Das, these VVIPs had to sit in Pangat with the common man, partake the same food and then and then only they were allowed to call on the Guru. Thus Pangat added a secular dimension to the concept of Sangat thereby eliminating the immoral evil practice of untouchability amongst the Hindus. The above two ingredients of Sikh organizational set up together with the spirit of *Simran* – participation in daily religious service – and *Seva* (service to the community in whatever form) resulted in strong bonds between members of the congregation.

A succession of ten Gurus embodying the same spirit, is a unique feature of Sikhism. The "one Spirit" in ten different personalities spread over a period of time is analogous to the institution of Dalai Lamas of Tibet, partially if not completely. Moreover, just as the Dalai Lamas are numbered First to Fourteenth, so are the Gurus – Nanak I to Nanak X. The doctrines of karma and transmigration are also part of the Sikh beliefs. Birth and rebirth fall in the same category. The similarities on fundamentals are much too pronounced to be ignored. One is therefore led to the inevitable conclusion that the principle of incarnation, if stripped of the aura of 'avatār', is as much a part of Sikh dharma as it is of Tibeto-Buddhism, or even Hinduism for that matter.

A true avatār of God Himself is not born in the human sense of the word. Like some well documented and researched cases of human beings having had many past lives, the Hindu avatārs of God Almighty also claim that they had many past lives of which they were aware of. It is a different matter altogether that other human beings are not aware of their past lives. Again, that does not mean that God is born. No, like our Sikh Gurus, He too is unborn, so says the Lord in Bhagavad Gītā:

> Many births have been left behind by Me and by thee, O Arjuna.
> I know them all, but thou knowest not…
>
> (IV: 5)
>
> "I am unborn, and My self is imperishable.… I come into being through My own Power (*māyā*)."
>
> (IV: 6)

A word of caution: In the foregoing discussion the distinction between 'incarnation' and 'reincarnation' must not be lost sight of. None of the Sikh Gurus were reincarnation of their predecessor; not by any stretch of imagination. On the contrary they were independent individual personalities, occupying the *Guru-Gaddi* in their own right, and not by virtue of the preceding Guru.

Convergence of Sikh Philosophical Thoughts

16

Initially, Sikhism was an off-shoot of Hinduism. For all practical purposes it was a sort of military organization to protect the non-Muslim public of India from the atrocities being perpetrated on them by the Muslim invaders from the North-West, and to prevent their forcible conversion to Islam. The *modus operandi* to attain that noble aim was not to use military means only, but to preach the noble thoughts of peaceful co-existence and communal harmony between the two antagonistic communities. After all, the Muslims of India were 'sons of the soil' with the microscopic exception of the invading hordes. Non-violence was the principal 'weapon' of restoring confidence and harmony. It is a moot point whether this ideology resolved the controversial issues in any worthwhile manner. In any case this aspect is more political than philosophical, and hence lies outside the scope of this work.

Guru Nanak's favorite metaphor is common to Upaniṣads and Hindu philosophical thought – he describes this world as an ocean, and liberation from it means to ferry the soul across to safety. The origin of this thought and metaphor may lie in Buddhism. It was only after the JOT, the Divine Light was installed in him by Nanak One that people bowed to Guru Angad. Thus, Sikhs did not bow to the human body but to the JOT that was installed in that person. The principle of Tibeto-Buddhist incarnation as applied to the line of Dalai Lamas is implied in the lineage of Sikh Gurus, without saying so in so many words. The Divine Light is the same, so are the 'Way and Mode' but the Master has only changed the body. Baba Nanak preached the Islamic belief in one God and that Muhammad is His messenger. Guru Nanak's teaching about God is summed in the Sikh 'Mūl Mantra', the creedal statement of Sikhism – '*Ek Onkar*', which stands for one primal reality. It is the equivalent of the Hindu 'OM' as in Kath Upaniṣad. Legend has it that when Nanak One left for his 'heavenly abode', no one found his body. Guru Nanak was not a mere human body; it was a JOT, a Divine Light, and his followers therefore could not find his mortal remains. A streak of Hindu/Buddhist Tantric belief is perceptible; hence the Guru's Mūl Mantra – Timeless and Formless, beyond birth and death.

The earth and the heavens shall perish; only He, the only One, remains for ever. After all, there is no other place to go except God; He is but One. These stanzas from the Adi Granth are a reflection of Guru Nanak's depth of understanding of Upaniṣads, Bhagavad Gītā and Islamic scriptures. It will thus be seen that the present differences between Sikhs and Muslims stem more from socio-political grounds and the tragic events of 1947 rather than on theological considerations.

Guru Nanak was a mystic. He searched for God within himself. The Christian-Protestant Mysticism believes that Divine Life and Light are within the man himself. "The Kingdom of God is within you and he who searches for it outside of himself will never find it.... God is within us and is waiting for us to return to Him." Guru Nanak always stressed cleansing of the inner self; he preached simple living and high thinking. Incarnation need not necessarily be restricted to God taking the form of Man; it could be incarnation of one man unto another. It is in this Tibeto-Buddhist context that the doctrine of incarnation may be considered applicable in Sikhism; and hence to Nanak I to Nanak X. Nevertheless, Sikhism is a strictly monotheistic system, and so is Christianity too.

> "The Self (*Ātman*) is existence, knowledge and bliss". The Ātman is universal and infinite. "There is no Hindu and there is no Mussalman; he who deems that both the ways lead to the one Lord, shall be emancipated."

The Fifth Nanak, Guru Arjan Dev, created an ocean of Holy Scripture called "Adi Granth". By virtue of its universal character, it was certainly "not a bible for the Sikhs alone", nor was it a life history of the Sikh Gurus; in fact, it contains Universal Truth "each and every word of which is dedicated to the Glory of the Almighty God only".

Guru Nanak discarded asceticism as a form of '*tapasya*'. Instead, he made normal household life as an essential pre-requisite for mystic training. Enforcement of differential symbolic features designed to make all Sikhs look distinctly different from Hindus and Muslims was yet another profound development.

Nām, the Divine Name, gives form to everything and through Nām comes Wisdom or Light. He who imbibes Nām reaches the highest state of development. Nām is '*Amrit*' – another variant of 'Bhakti Yoga'. The concept of *Haumain* came into being while the fatalistic strains of Doctrine of Karma were discarded. Karma was adopted as a positive feature of a person's life. The Concept of Guruship was refined and codified while the principle of succession for the nine Gurus after Baba Nanak was a modified form of Tibeto-Buddhist concept of Doctrine of Reincarnation, albeit much different. Similarly, the Doctrine of Transmigration was adopted, but with very little modifications. Birth and rebirth fall in the same category. The transformation from one Guru to the next took place in the same way as one lamp is lit from another. It was the same holy light carried through, the same "Divine Flame in continuity of the same Divine Mission", each one incarnation of the previous one, from the beginning to the end, from the First Guru to the Tenth Guru. Every Dalai Lama had a distinct name; so did every Guru. Every Dalai Lama was distinguished by his serial number – one to fourteen; so was every Guru of the Sikhs; from one to the Tenth. The analogy to Gyalwa Rinpoché, the Dalai Lama as One to Fourteen is much too obvious to require any emphasis. Similarly, as in Tibeto-Buddhism, in Sikhism too a man is called upon to "accept the Will of God and thus sublimate his suffering and loss" trusting in conquest of sorrow and suffering through ceaseless endeavor. Although Sikhism was an offshoot of Hinduism and philosophically much closer to the latter, it followed in the footsteps of modified form of Buddhism as followed in Tibet, giving rise to the title of "Nanak Lama".

The similarities on fundamentals are much too pronounced to be ignored. One is, therefore, led to the inevitable conclusion that the principle of incarnation, if stripped of the aura of 'avatār', is as much a part of Sikh dharma as it is of Tibeto-Buddhism, or even

Hinduism for that matter. It is a different matter altogether that other human beings are not aware of their past lives. Again, that does not mean that God is born. No, like our Sikh Gurus, He too is unborn, so says the Lord in Bhagavad Gītā – "I am unborn, and Myself is imperishable. I come into being through My own Power (*māyā*)."

Select Bibliography

Anand, Balwant Singh: *Guru Nanak*; Guru Nanak Foundation; New Delhi.

Bal, Sarjit Singh (ed.): *Guru Nanak in the Eyes of Non-Sikhs*; Panjab University, Chandigarh.

Cole, Owen W.: *Sikhism and its Indian Context 1479-1708*; Darton, Longman & Todd, London, 1984.

Grewal, J.S. & Indu Bagga (ed.): *The Khalsa Over 300 Years*; Tulika, New Delhi, 1999.

Grewal, J.S.: *Guru Nanak in History*; Panjab University, Chandigarh.

Karnaratna, S.W.: *Guru Nanak and Ceylon*; Punjabi University, Patiala.

Kaushik, Sarup Singh: *Guru kian Saakhian*; Singh Brothers, Amritsar.

Khan Mohammad Waliullah Khan: *Sikh Shrines in West Pakistan.*

Khazan Singh: *History and Philosophy of Sikh Religion*; Lahore, 1969.

Kohli, Surinder Singh: *Travels of Guru Nanak*; Panjab University, Chandigarh, 1969/77.

Loehlin, C.H.: *The Sikhs and Their Scriptures*, Lucknow Publishing House, 1964.

Macauliffe, M.A.: *The Sikh Religion*, Six Vols.; Delhi.

Macleod, W.H.: *Guru Nanak and Sikh Religion*, Princeton and Oxford, 1968.

– – : *Early Sikh Tradition*; Clarendon Press, Oxford, 1980.

– – : *Exploring Sikhism*; Oxford University Press, 2000.

Mann, Arjan Singh: *Guru Tegh Bahadur and Assam.*

Singh, Daljit: *SIKHISM: A Comparative Study of Its Theology and Mysticism;* Amritsar, 1994.

Singh, Dr. Gopal: *A History of the Sikh People*; Allied Publishers, Mumbai, 1988/2005.

– – : *The Religion of the Sikhs*; Allied Publishers, Mumbai, Amritsar, 1994.

Singh, Dr. Kirpal: *Janamsakhi Tradition*; Singh Brothers, Amritsar, 2004.

Singh, Ganda (ed.): *Sources on the Life and Teachings of Guru Nanak*; Punjabi University, Patiala; 1969.

Singh, Harbans: *Guru Nanak and the Origins of the Sikh Faith*; Asia Publishing House; Bombay, 1969.

Singh, Khushwant: *A History of the Sikhs*, Two Vols.; Oxford University Press, 1977/2006.

Singh, Tarcholan: *Guru Nanak, Founder of Sikhism*; GPC, Sis Ganj, Delhi.

Singh: *Guru Nanak*; Guru Nanak Foundation; New Delhi.

Trump, Ernest: *The Adi Granth*; New Delhi, 1970.

Tulku, Tarunga: Similarities Between Sikhism and Buddhism; *Indian Times*; Delhi.

Vir Singh, Bhai: *Guru Nanak Chamatkar*; Two Vols.; 1988/2005.

– – : *The Religion of the Sikhs*; Allied Publishers, Mumbai, Amritsar, 1994.